Flying against the Wind

BY

Ina R. Friedman

Also by Ina R. Friedman

*The Other Victims: First Person Stories of
    Non-Jews Persecuted by the Nazis*

*Escape or Die: True Stories of Young People
    Who Survived the Holocaust*

Black Cop

How My Parents Learned to Eat

Art, Cover Illustrations &
design by Michael Lenn
with Futura Condensed for Display
and Concorde for Text

Production by Robert B. Smyth

Flying against the Wind

THE STORY OF A YOUNG WOMAN
WHO DEFIED THE NAZIS

BY

INA R. FRIEDMAN

Lodgepole Press
Brookline, Massachusetts

Published by Lodgepole Press, 1995,
Brookline, Massachusetts, United States of America.

Photo Credits:

1.) Page 9: Amelie Breling. 2.) Pages 14 & 23: Akademie der Wissenschaften, Berlin, Germany. 3.) Page 41: United States Holocaust Memorial Museum. 4.) Page 47: John Fletcher/Bettmann Archives. 5.) Page 58: United States Holocaust Memorial Museum. 6.) Pages 86 & 87: Eric Politzer/Leo Baeck Institute. 7.) Pages 104 & 105: Owen Franken/German Information Center. 8.) Pages 129 & 179: Akademie der Wissenschaften, Berlin, Germany.

Library of Congress Cataloging-in-Publication Data
Friedman, Ina R.
Flying against the Wind: The Story of a Young Woman
Who Defied the Nazis /Ina R. Friedman.
Includes chronology, glossary, bibliographical references, and index.
Summary: Biography of one of the few young Germans to resist the Nazis and the story of growing up in Nazi Germany before and during World War II.
ISBN 1-886721-00-9
LCCP 94-073664

1. World War II, 1939-1943–Juvenile/young adult Biography-literature.
2. Resistance in Germany, World War II, 1939-1943–Juvenile/young adult literature 3. Feminist literature–Juvenile/young adult. 4. History-World War II–Juvenile/young adult. 5. Youth in Europe–Juvenile/young adult literature-Biography 6. Righteous gentiles–Europe, World War II. 7. Holocaust–Resistance to in Germany.

For information contact:
Lodgepole Press
PO Box 1259
Brookline, MA 02146
(617) 277-2323
Fax: 617-277-4592

IN MEMORY OF
OLGA AND AMELIE

TWO WOMEN OF COURAGE

Table Of Contents

Acknowledgements

This biography of Cato Bontjes van Beek was drawn from her letters and diary; from interviews with her sister and confidant, Meme (Mietje,) her mother Olga, and from her cousins Maria Schmidt Sparano, Marianne Schulze-Ritter von Randow, and other family members.

In England, I interviewed Cato's childhood friend, Annita Otterstedt Oldnall; Pat Beesley Finch, with whom she stayed during her visit to Great Britain in 1937; and John Hall, her English boyfriend. Detta and Hannes Lange, friends from Berlin, added further details.

I am indebted to historian Heinz Hoehne for the use of his files on the Red Orchestra, the Russian spy ring. My thanks, too, to Regina Griebel of the Akademie der Wissenschaften (formerly of the DDR,) Zentralinstitut für Geschichte, who supplied me with documents, photographs, copies of Cato's letters, and other pertinent material.

Special acknowledgment is due to Stella Belovin for introducing me to the Bontjes van Beeks and to Sam Starobin for serving as interpreter during the many interviews I conducted in Germany and for the hours he spent translating documents and letters.

My thanks, too, to Suzi Bolotin, Jesse Friedman, Rabbi Ronne Friedman, Phyllis Goldstein of Facing History, Dr. Dan Hade of

the Pennsylvania State University, Elaine
Reisman, Barbara Roberts, Dr. Margot Stern
Strom, director of Facing History; Annie Thompson, and Sonia Weitz, director of the Holocaust
Center of the North Shore; for reading the
manuscript. Vivian Boxer of the photographic
department of the United States Holocaust
Memorial Museum was most helpful in locating
photographs. I am grateful to Mike and Rhoda
Abrams, Thelma and Michael Gruenbaum,
Ingrid and Roy Kisliuk, and Natalie Rothstein for
their support and to my copy editor, Roberta
Winston, and to Robert B. Smyth for their insights and skills in the preparation of this book.
My apologies to anyone I inadvertently omitted.

The photographs in *Flying against the Wind*
are from the Akademie der Wissenschaften, The
United States Holocaust Memorial Museum, and
Owen Franken/German Information Center.

List of Characters

FAMILY

Cato (Kah-TOW) Bontjes van Beek, nicknamed Dodo

Olga Breling Bontjes van Beek, her mother, a dancer, musician and artist

Jan Bontjes van Beek, her father, a ceramicist

Mietje (MEET-jchee), or Meme, Bontjes van Beek, her younger sister

Tim Bontjes van Beek, her younger brother

GRANDPARENTS:

Heinrich Breling, (Grossvater,) an artist

Amalie Mayer Breling, (Grossmutter,) a musician

AUNTS AND UNCLES:

Amelie Breling, a ceramicist

Emma Breling, an interpreter and business woman

Jossi Breling Schultze-Ritter, a composer

Hans Schultze-Ritter, a conductor

Lolo Breling Modersohn, an artist

Otto Modersohn, an artist

Haina Breling Schmidt, a weaver

Fritz Schmidt, a ceramicist and electrician

COUSINS:

Ulrich & Christian Modersohn, sons of Lolo and Otto Modersohn

Maria & Olga Schmidt, daughters of Haina and Fritz Schmidt

Marianne Schultze-Ritter, daughter of Jossi and Hans Schultze-Ritter

Villagers:

Annita and Aennee Otterstedt, childhood friends
Pastor Tidow, anti-Nazi minister
Heinrich Peper, *gauleiter,* (Nazi administrator) of the local district

The Men Who Loved Her:

John Hall, an Englishman
Hannes Lange, a medical student
Heinz Strelow, a soldier and journalist
Helmut Nievert, an S.S. officer

Friends and Foes:

The Beesleys of Grete-Wynchcombe, England
Rali Bontjes van Beek, her stepmother
Theodor Lessing, family friend and philosopher
Eva Rittmeister, an actress who was active in the resistance
Dr. John Rittmeister, Eva's husband, and a psychiatrist who was active in the resistance
Detta Zimmerman, friend who aided French prisoners of war
Libertas Schulze-Boysen, film specialist and member of the anti-Nazi spy ring, the Red Orchestra
Harro Schulze-Boysen, Libertas husband, head of the German branch of the The Red Orchestra
Manfred Roeder, "the Butcher of Berlin," a prosecutor
Reverend Augustus Ohm, pastor, Ploetzensee Prison

Chapter 1
Berlin
Alexanderplatz Prison
March 1943

C ato stood beneath the tiny barred window just below the ceiling of her cell. On tip-toe, she retrieved the flower Mama had put on top of the clean laundry she brought to the prison each week. Cato had placed the precious flower on the ledge so it could live as long as possible in the fresh air and sunlight. Gently, she touched the flower to her cheek.

She had asked for the flower in the note she inserted in the seam of her pajamas. Mama picked up the wash from a special window each week, returning it, neatly wrapped in newspaper. Today, the tulip lay on top.

Shivering, Cato turned toward the unlighted cell. For weeks, her fingers explored the walls, hoping to find a crevice through which she could whisper to another human being.

She knew there were others. At mealtime, she heard the click as the guard opened the cell.

During the day, with the light from the barred window, Cato was filled with hope, reassuring her mother in her letters that the death sentence would not be carried out.

But at night, the blackness entombed her, intensifying every sound–the piercing wail of the air raid sirens, the scratch of the rats as they raced toward her bed, the screams from a racked soul. Every odor–the musty smell of her un-washed clothes–the stink from the slop bucket–while bearable during the day, rose up, clutching at her throat at night. She tried to escape into sleep. But the dampness magnified the cold. Beneath her threadbare blanket, Cato's frozen fingers reached out to crush the lice attacking her scalp, under her arms. Exhausted, she dozed, only to be awakened by nightmares.

At dawn, she rose and turned once more to the window. As the sky brightened, Cato thought it looked incredibly blue, with huge pillows of white clouds appearing and disappearing above the narrow window. It was the same sky she had loved when she wandered through the fields of Fischerhude.

Was it really six and a half weeks since she had been sentenced to death? It seemed unreal, to wait each day, hoping that the sentence would be reduced to life in prison, and at the same time, trying to reconcile herself to the possibility that at any moment the door would open and the executioner would enter?

How did it happen that she, Cato Bontjes van Beek, only twenty-two years old, who loved Germany–truly loved it–now stood in this cell, condemned to death as a spy, waiting each day to discover if she would live or die?

Cato thought longingly of Fischerhude, the tiny farming village in northern Germany where she had been born. It had always seemed to her to be the most wonderful place in the world. The minute the teacher dismissed them from school, Cato, her younger sister, Mietje, her little brother, Tim, and their cousin Maria Schmidt would take off their wooden shoes and run barefoot across the dirt road, between the tombstones in the churchyard and down the lane, past cows grazing in the fields, to their house overlooking the Wuemme River.

Seven rivers flowed across the flat moorlands. No mild day passed without Cato, Mietje, Tim, and Maria hopping into the water. Ducks and geese squawked and scattered as the children swam back and forth. Sometimes they would hop out and explore the shady forests on the other side of the river. When they returned home, the youngsters sprawled on the foot-high sand dune—their "mountain"—at the rear of the house. Cato, the oldest, would tell them stories.

Who could have known that the very qualities that had made others treasure and admire her— her intelligence, curiosity, courage, and passion for justice—would have brought her here, alone in this cell, facing an end to a life that had held so many dreams?

Once more, as had been her practice since her arrest, her voice rose in song—to give courage to herself and to the other prisoners, "Let the whole creation cry, glory to the Lord on high."

PART I
CHILD OF FIELD AND STREAM

1920-1935

CHAPTER 2

The Family

E ven as a child, Cato Bontjes van Beek knew her family was different from the other families in Fischerhude, a tiny village in northern Germany. Unlike their neighbors, who were farmers, her parents and aunts and uncles were artists and musicians.

But what else could one expect of a family that in the eyes of Cato and her younger sister, Mietje, began with a fairy tale?

In her diary, Mietje tells the story,

> Once upon a time, there was a small boy who tended geese . . .

> With little to do except watch the fowl glide up and down the river, he began to sketch, on scraps of paper, the people and houses of his village. A Jewish storekeeper saw the young boy's drawings and showed them to an agent of the king of Hannover.

> The king summoned the twelve year old boy to his court and enrolled him in a gymnasium, or German high school. When the boy graduated, the

king sent him to the Academy of Art
in Munich. There, King Ludwig II of
Bavaria saw the young man's work
and appointed him Royal Painter.

"When the king died, the famous artist returned to his village of Fischerhude, and with
him," Mietje adds, "his wife, Amalie, and their six
lovely daughters, of whom the youngest is my
mother, Olga. A fairy tale? And yet true. This
small boy who once herded geese was my grandfather, Heinrich Breling."

On his return to Fischerhude, Heinrich Breling
built a house in the meadow overlooking the
Wuemme River. Following the North German
custom, he placed two wooden horses, symbols
of the god Wotan, on each end of the roof for
good luck.

Other artists settled nearby, and famous musicians, writers, artists, and philosophers came
from all over Germany to enjoy the country air
and the Breling's hospitality.

They brought with them new ideas in art,
music, and literature, as well as talk of the political situation. Heinrich Breling, who encouraged
his six daughters to draw, and Amalie Breling,
who taught them to sing and to play the piano,
encouraged the young women to take part in
these discussions.

Frequently there was more than music coming
from the open windows. Each daughter, abso-
lutely certain that her opinion was the correct

one, attempted to shout down her sisters. It was from their mother they got their fiery temperament. For Grossmutter, as her grandchildren called her, frequently became so excited she banged her fist on the kitchen table to make a point.

This freedom to speak out and explore new ideas shocked the villagers. In the late nine-

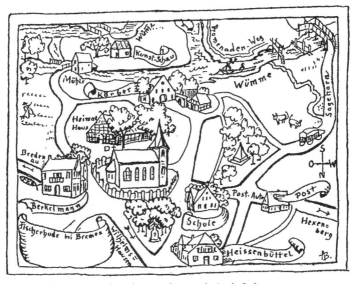

A drawing of Fischerhude in the early twentieth century by Amelie Breling.

teenth century, properly raised young women were taught to curtsy to adults while looking only at their feet, keep house, and be silent when menfolk discussed business or politics. The Breling sisters not only had opinions but traveled abroad to pursue careers.

Amelie, the eldest, apprenticed to the sculptor Maillol in Paris.

Lolo, the most tempetuous, first set out to be an opera singer, then turned to painting; Jossi studied music and became a composer; Haina, a weaver; and Emma traveled before World War I to England and across Russia to become an interpreter.

Cato's mother, Olga, studied modern dance with Sandy and Isadora Duncan in Darmstadt, Germany.

Because Heinrich Breling had brought great honor to the village, the "Professor's Kinder," as his daughters and later his grandchildren were called, were treated with respect.   Still, they were looked upon as "different."

Heinrich Breling died in 1914, but his independent spirit was passed down to his grandchildren.

It was into this warm, noisy, and exciting family that Cato Bontjes van Beek, the daughter of Olga Breling and Jan Bontjes van Beek, was born on November 14, 1920.

Chapter 3

A Very Unusual Papa

C ato was in trouble again. She hadn't meant to be, but like the other times, it just happened. The morning had begun like every other morning, with five-year-old Cato telling three-year-old Mietje and their six-year-old cousin Marianne their plans for the day—Cowboys and Indians.

Her father, Jan, laughed and invited the girls into his studio for "war paint." With stripes of purple, red, and orange paint on their arms, foreheads, and chests, the three ran outside. Cato stuck chicken feathers in their blond hair and handed them the bows and arrows she had made from twigs and string.

A huge chestnut tree stood to the right of the back porch. Since Tim was only a year old, Cato put him at the bottom of the tree as their papoose. Cato was unusually large and well coordinated for her age and quickly scampered to the uppermost branch. Small and wiry Marianne, who was visiting from Berlin, soon joined her. But Mietje could reach only the lowest limb.

From their perch, Cato and Marianne overlooked the meadow surrounding the house and the woods on the other side of the river. Far away, they could see cows grazing and a thin trail of smoke from the brick kiln in the neighboring town of Ottersberg. A few children in hollowed-out logs drifted down the Wuemme.

Cato's mother, Olga, sat on the back porch painting the yellow daisies carpeting the meadows. It was a typical July day, with fleecy white clouds slowly drifting across the blue sky.

As the girls climbed from one branch to another, their faces turned red and dripped with sweat. Wiping her face on her sleeve, Cato told Mietje and Marianne, "Indians don't wear clothes. So we don't have to either." Gleefully, the girls tossed their dresses and underpants to the ground.

A neighbor spotted them swinging from branch to branch. Indignant, she stormed onto the porch, interrupting Olga at her easel.

After the woman left, Olga called the children to come down and put on their clothes. Cato was furious. "Just because of that silly old woman," she argued, "we have to put on sweaty dresses. It's not fair."

"I told her," Olga says, "'there's nothing wrong with going naked, but we don't want to offend the neighbors.'"

Cato's independence and creativity came as much from her father, Jan Bontjes, as it did from the Breling side of the family. By the time he was twelve, he could play eight musical instruments, as well as sing, dance, and draw.

Though Jan was born in Holland, his father had immigrated to Germany when Jan was a child. As a teenager, Jan rebelled and ran off to join the German navy during World War I.

By November 1918, Germany knew it had lost the war and agreed to sign an armistice to end the fighting on November 11. Despite the war coming to an end, the German admirals decided to send their ships out to sea for "one last glorious battle."

Jan and his shipmates saw no point in being killed to add a medal to an admiral's chest. They rebelled. The ships remained in port. From that time on, Jan became known as "Der Rote Matrossa," the Red Sailor, since the Germans felt that only Communists (Reds) would refuse to obey an order, however senseless.

After the war, Jan and his shipmate, Fritz Schmidt, came to an artists' colony in nearby Worpswede. The first time Olga saw him, he was standing on top of a hay wagon. "With the sun shining on his blond hair, he looked like a god," she recalls. "Tall, broad-shouldered, and very handsome."

In a short time, they were married. But with all his talents, Jan could not find a job. "So I taught him to dance," Olga says "But he couldn't stand the dust and makeup of the theater. I sent him home to my mother and sister Amelie, to see if they could help him."

Since Jan was artistic, Amelie, who was a sculptor and ceramicist, taught him to make ceramics. Fritz Schmidt, who had married Haina Breling, was also creative. The three formed the Fischerhude Ceramic Company and set up a workshop in Heinrich Breling's former studio.

When Olga became pregnant with Cato, she had to stop dancing. Since she and Jan could not afford to rent an apartment, they moved in with Amelie and Grossmutter.

Cato Bontjes van Beek at the age of three.

As elsewhere in Germany, the family found it hard to earn a living. After the war, the country had to pay huge sums of money for the farms and industries and homes the German army destroyed in northern France. These payments impoverished Germany and left the nation without money to restart industries. Jobless and hungry veterans roamed the cities seeking work, and every day hundreds of homeless people collapsed from starvation.

In Fischerhude, few people had money to buy ceramic dishes, and Olga was grateful that their neighbors were willing to trade milk, potatoes, cabbages, and eggs in exchange for ceramic plates and cups. Though the Bontjes-Breling household had enough to eat, there was no money for new clothes or leather shoes.

Jan resented having to wear pants with patches and wooden shoes. His leather shoes had to be saved for the trips he made to Berlin or Bremen to sell their wares. His father had been an engineer, and Jan was used to a bountiful table, not an endless diet of potatoes and cabbage.

To Jan, young and dreaming of becoming a famous ceramicist, living in Fischerhude was like walking around in a straightjacket.

By the time Mietje, later Meme, was born on May 6, 1922, the family's fortunes had not improved, and the country had sunken deeper and deeper into a depression.

That year, the government ran out of cash, and it began to print more and more money to pay its bills. The result was a wild inflation. A loaf of bread that sold for a few marks quickly rose in price to a thousand, then a million, and later a billion marks. People carried their money to the store in potato sacks just to buy one loaf of bread.

Unaware of their poverty, Cato and Mietje thought Fischerhude a paradise. They gobbled up potatoes and cabbage soup and asked for more.

But for Olga, it was difficult. When it was time for her to give birth to Tim, there was no money to go to the hospital in Bremen. The reddish-blond-haired baby was born on August 26, 1924, at home.

Through the years, friends continued to visit from all over Germany and Europe. These writers, artists, and musicians came bearing magazines and books on art, literature, and music. Cato grabbed them and ran into the garden.

In the evenings, after the nightly concerts, talk of politics resounded across the living room, bounced off the walls of the kitchen, and echoed through the garden. The grand jumble of opinions, questions, laughter, and discussion fascinated Cato and Mietje. Encouraged by their parents, the Bontjes children spoke up, unafraid to ask questions of Germany's most prominent writers and philosophers.

Most of the family's friends were liberals and freethinkers. Many were Jews. Whenever they talked about Adolf Hitler, the leader of the Nationalist Socialist German Workers party, fear clouded their faces. Hitler blamed the Jews, not the generals, for Germany losing World War 1 and promised to drive the Jews out of Germany.

Following World War 1, Germany's democratic government, led by the Social Democrats, was weak. Right-wing political parties, such as the German Nationalist and the National Socialist German Workers Parties, thought violence was the only way to change the government.

It was at this chaotic time that Hitler, a former corporal in the German army, joined the then insignificant party, the National Socialist German Workers party, and started the Nazi movement. Storm Troopers, Hitler's private police force, interrupted the meetings of other political organizations and murdered their leaders.

In their brown shirts, brown pants, and black boots, the Storm Troopers swaggered down the middle of streets singing the "Horst Wessel." Anyone who did not salute or get out of the way was beaten up. People ducked into doorways to avoid having to acknowledge the "Brownshirts."

While Cato thought they were disgusting, her teenage cousin, Ulrich Modersohn, did not. One evening, after Olga and Tim finished playing a duet, Ulrich announced that when he was twenty-one, he would join the Storm Troopers.

Everyone was stunned. Amelie, never at a loss for words, berated him. "The man is evil. He'll lead us into another bloody war."

"No! Hitler will lead us to glory!" Ulrich shouted. "He's our only hope."

It was incomprehensible to Cato that her beloved cousin would want to become a Storm Trooper. Gentle Ulrich! When she was small, he used to carry her on his shoulders, letting her peek into birds' nests. Ulrich, who spent hours discussing art and poetry with them, now wanting to march with the Brownshirts? Ulrich, part man, part boy, still joined the Bontjes children in their stickball games. In the winter, he ice-skated with them. Easter was always a wonderful time, with Ulrich leading their search for elaborately decorated eggs.

Ulrich and his younger brother, Christian, were the sons of Lolo and Otto Modersohn, and every girl in the village had a crush on the strapping, broad-shouldered, blue-eyed young men. Both dreamed of becoming artists like their father, Otto Modersohn, and their grandfather, Heinrich Breling. Now, Ulrich was turning against everything the family had tried to teach him. He argued that the Nazi way, despite its hatred and brutality, was the only way for Germany.

But the more his mother, Lolo, and Amelie, Cato, Mietje, Tim, and everyone else in the family tried to change his mind, the more adamant Ulrich became.

"There were frequent fights between Amelie and Ulrich," Mietje recounts, "but it never got to the point where Amelie drove him out of the house. He was family."

Like Ulrich, the other boys in the village, most of whom worked on farms for low wages, turned to Hitler and his promise of prosperity. Alarmed, Fritz and Jan, over a glass of schnapps in the local *gasthaus*, tried to convince their neighbors that Hitler would only lead them into war. And Amelie, before the elections, urged her neighbors not to vote for the Nazis.

Few wanted to listen. Cato began to see more and more swastikas, the Nazi symbol, on the sides of barns and in the lapels of the farmers as they walked to church on Sunday. As she listened to her parents talk about the Nazis, Cato detected an increasing fear in their voices that Hitler might win the election.

For the first time, Cato became aware that her family could be in trouble if the Nazis took over Germany.

CHAPTER 4

Another Fairy Tale?

As impossible as it seemed, Cato was trying to balance an umbrella on the bridge of her nose. She had been thinking about the trick all day. When the school bell rang, she dashed outside to the school yard. She opened the umbrella. It teetered on her nose for a few moments, and then fell to the ground. Everyone laughed as Cato picked up the umbrella and, imitating the actor Charlie Chaplin, walked splayfooted down the dirt road.

The Fischerhude schoolhouse had only two rooms. In one, a teacher taught the first, second, and third grades. In the other, a schoolmaster instructed the fourth, fifth, and sixth grades. Cato, with her quick mind, grew impatient with the slow pace of learning. She always wanted to know more.

Whenever she raised her hand to ask a question, the teacher got angry. Rather than feel his switch on her hands, she kept quiet and began to think about amusing things to do after school. Sometimes Cato, Mietje, Tim, and their cousin Maria Schmidt would float downstream in a borrowed boat to Ottersberg and wander in the woods. But usually Cato planned a play for Mietje, Tim, and Maria to act out on their "mountain." The "mountain" was a small dune, three feet high, beside the Wuemme.

After they rehearsed on the "mountain," the children climbed the stairs to the attic to rummage through an old leather trunk for costumes. Inside the trunk, which they nicknamed "Hannibal's Coffers," were Grandfather Breling's old tuxedo, cape, and top hat—and the satin and velvet gowns Grossmutter wore when she twirled across the ballrooms of King Ludwig's palaces.

Cato had no difficulty finding plots for her plays. Unlike in most homes, where the only book was a Bible, in Cato's house, the shelves were crammed with fairy tales, myths, geographies, histories, books on philosophy, even books in foreign languages. To Cato, each cover held a mystery. She had to know what was inside.

In 1931, Cato's "perfect" world began to fall apart. To sell their ceramics, Jan began to spend a great deal of time traveling to big cities: Berlin, Cologne, Prague. Wherever he went, he made friends, joining them for a schnapps in the local cabarets and theaters. When he returned, he taught the family the latest songs, showing off the newest dances, like the foxtrot and the two-step. Cato was the first to jump up and dance around the floor with her father.

But despite his good humor, Jan was unhappy. He tried to explain to Olga that living in Fischerhude stiffled him as an artist. He needed the stimulation of a big city where he could come in contact with other artists and musicians every day.

But Olga couldn't see abandoning Fischerhude for the insecurity of a big city. When Jan insisted, as painful as it was, she suggested a divorce.

Cato couldn't understand. Mama and Papa loved each other. How could they even think about a divorce? With tears, Cato watched Jan pack up his battered suitcase and walk down the road toward the station.

Olga Bontjes van Beek with Cato, Meme, and Tim.

To make her twelve-year-old's world even more confusing, Ulrich continued to praise Hitler. Cato tried to argue with him, pointing out that if elected, Hitler would imprison, even murder, many of the family's friends, the very same people whose music and art and conversation Ulrich enjoyed.

"Under Hitler," Ulrich told her stiffly, "individuals will not count. Everything will be done for the good of the state."

Distressed, Cato asked Olga how Ulrich, a member of *their* family, could turn into a parrot, repeating over and over again Nazi garbage.

"I told her," Olga recalls, "'Ulrich wants to believe in a master race. When he looks in the mirror, he sees the perfect Aryan described by Hitler: a tall, blond-haired, blue-eyed superman. It gives him a feeling of power.'"

Cato shook her head. It was difficult to accept her mother's explanation. Childlike, she wanted to believe that eventually everything, like a fairy tale, would turn out all right—her father would return to Fischerhude, and Ulrich would stop being a Nazi.

Chapter 5

Heroines and Heroes

B ut Cato's concerns did not stop her from exploring new possibilities. Suddenly women could fly! For in the spring of 1932, Amelia Earhart became the first woman to solo across the Atlantic.

A few days later, Cato rushed out of school and pulled out a diagram from her backpack. Placing it on the ground, she showed Mietje, Maria, and Tim the details of the plane they would build on their "mountain." Instead of going home for a snack, they ran to the sand dune and began to scoop out a "cockpit."

"Then she had us scouring the village for equipment," Maria relates. The wheels of two discarded wheelbarrows became steering wheels. With scraps of leather from Amelie's sewing basket, Mietje pieced together two pairs of goggles, one for Cato, the pilot, and one for Tim, the copilot. Behind Winkelmann's general store, Mietje found four abandoned crates for seats. Cato turned tin cans and door handles into mock controls.

When the control panel was finished, Mietje and Maria sat in the back as passengers as Cato and Tim piloted the plane.

Every evening, Cato pored over the geography books, plotting the next day's journey. As she "flew" across the world, Cato told her passengers which rivers they passed, the names of the mountains, how the people were dressed, and the languages they spoke.

In a house filled with love, art, music, and conversation, Olga and Amelie believed in letting children pursue their dreams. Mietje's was to become a famous artist. Tim, at an early age, was determined to become a concert pianist. Now Cato wanted to be a pilot as well as an actress.

Cato's fascination with flying increased when Hans Bertram, a German flier, took off from Cologne for Australia in February, 1933. This was a daring venture in a seaplane, the *Atlantis*. In those days, a plane could carry only a small amount of gasoline and had to make frequent landings to refuel.

Since they couldn't afford a penny for a newspaper, Cato, her arms wrapped around her knees, sat spellbound each night in front of the radio listening to the reports of Bertram's progress from country to country: Cologne to Lake Constance . . . over the Alps and across the Mediterranean Sea . . . high above the Syrian desert, Persia, India, Asia . . .

Bertram's picture hung over her iron bedstead, along with photos of Amelia Earhart and movie stars Cary Grant, Greta Garbo, and Robert Taylor.

In her exuberance, Cato wrote a poem, which she set to music:

> Oh, my dear, my good Hans Bertram,
>
> Oh, if I could only see you one time, Hans Bertram!
>
> The whole world would I give you
>
> And also my young life.
>
> Oh, if only I could see you one time, Hans Bertram!

Bertram's sudden disappearance over the Australian desert frightened Cato. Every morning and before she went to bed, she turned on the radio, hoping for some news that her hero had been found. Two months passed before the announcer reported Bertram was alive. He had been found by aborigines and nursed back to health, and when he returned to Germany, he wrote a book about his adventures.

Cato longed for a copy, but she knew it was impossible. Since Papa left, there was even less money than before. But that Christmas, to Cato's delight, Olga scraped together enough money to buy her a copy. Cato read and reread the autobiography, quoting passages to Mietje and their best friend Annita until they put their hands over their ears.

It was a good thing Cato had the book as a diversion. For one terrifying event followed another when the Nazis took over Germany in January 1933.

Chapter 6

Lightning

Instead of jumping up as she usually did and imitating Hitler whenever she heard his voice, Cato sat paralyzed in front of the radio.

Moments before, President Hindenburg had announced Hitler's appointment as chancellor of Germany. None of the political parties had received a majority, but the Nazi party had received more votes than any others in the November 1932 election. Hindenburg then asked Hitler to form a coalition government. Hindenburg, the commanding general of the German army during World War I, thought he could control Hitler, a former corporal.

An unusual silence gripped the adults that day, January 30, 1933, as Grossmutter, Amelie, and Olga stood before the radio listening to Hitler's first broadcast as chancellor. His words, "One Nation, One People, One Leader" (*Ein Vaterland, Ein Volk, Ein Führer*), left them stunned.

Though there was a blazing fire in the tile oven, goose bumps raced up and down Cato's arms and legs. Even she knew "One Nation, One

People, One Leader" were code words—a warning that no disagreement would be tolerated. No political party, except the Nazi party, would be permitted. Anyone who was different—Jews, Communists, Social Democrats—or who said or did anything against Hitler was in danger. That included her family and their friends.

As Cato sat there, trying to imagine how this would affect her, she heard Amelie gasp, "Theodor!"

Professor Theodor Lessing, one of Germany's most distinguished philosophers, was a friend of Amelie's of long standing. The handsome man with a thick black beard was a frequent visitor to Fischerhude and, according to Tim, the children's favorite storyteller. On each visit, he took them into the garden, and under the chestnut tree his deep voice led them inside the enchanted world of Hans Christian Anderson, or to Roman and Greek myths, or to legends from the Bible.

For years, Professor Lessing wrote articles condemning the Nazis for their racial policies. As a liberal and as a Jew, he was in immediate danger. In her fear that he would be hunted down and murdered, Amelie sent him a message telling him to come to Fischerhude. They would hide him.

"It was a very courageous thing to do," Olga says. Anyone found hiding an "enemy of the people" could be sent to prison or executed.

As her mother stood trembling before the radio, Cato was only vaguely aware that her father and Uncle Fritz, because they were Social Democrats, and Amelie, who had spoken out against the Nazis, were in danger.

From the moment Hitler became chancellor, Storm Troopers, in police trucks and vans, raced through the streets of Germany. Screeching to a stop before the homes and offices of Communists, Social Democrats, editors, Jews, artists, and actors, the Nazis arrested those on blacklists, drawn up through the years, of anyone who opposed the Nazis. People were pulled from their apartments and murdered. Others were beaten and thrown into prisons or concentration camps.

Though Fritz and Jan and Amelie were not taken into "protective custody," they knew the police vans or a Gestapo limousine could stop at their doors at any time.

As the headlines boasted of more and more arrests of "traitors," the family awaited a reply from Professor Lessing. For three months they heard nothing. Then Amelie received a letter assuring her that he was safe in Marienbad, Czechoslovakia. "As Grossmutter always says," Lessing wrote, "everything will turn out all right."

By the end of February, Hitler had suspended the constitution of the Weimar Republic, abolishing the right of free speech and the right of assembly. Other political parties were abolished. Any voice raised against Hitler, whether on the radio, in the street, or in the press, led to imprisonment. Even words spoken in the home. Children were warned at school of their patriotic duty to report every remark critical of Hitler or the Nazis to the police.

Suddenly, the family that had encouraged free speech had to censor everything they said: at tea, or while shopping, walking to the village, or strolling along the Wuemme. Even the trees had ears. When Olga entered the church to play the organ, she limited her conversation to the weather, the parishoners' health, or the state of the crops.

Amelie and Olga admonished the children never to repeat any conversations that took place inside the house. Cato was told not to discuss with her classmates the books she read at home. Under Nazi law, books by foreign authors were subversive.

"Now began a perilous game," Mietje says, "when we had to learn to go about with unspoken thoughts." Undaunted, Cato made up a sign language which she shared with Tim, Mietje, Maria, and the miller's daughters, Annita and Aenne Otterstedt. The girls' parents had been against the Nazis before the election, and they could be trusted. Their fingers flying, they shared the jokes Cato made up about Hitler.

In March, the first concentration camp, Dachau, opened. Nobody knew what went on behind the barbed-wire compound, but the Nazis circulated rumors that terrible things happened inside. Even schoolchildren added a line to their prayers: "Lord, please let me be good so I won't go to Dachau."

Since the newspapers printed only what the Nazis wanted Germans to read, there was a hunger to know what was really happening. The only solution was to listen to shortwave radio, which was forbidden. If discovered, Amelie and Olga could be put in jail for tuning to Radio Orange, the Dutch station, or to BBC, the British Broadcasting Corporation.

At broadcast time, Cato stood by the front door, Tim at the living room window, and Mietje at the kitchen door to signal if anyone was coming up the path. Olga and Amelie huddled close to the radio. A quick shout, "Someone's coming," made them turn off the radio and cover it with a cloth.

One evening in August, as Cato stood watch at the front door, she heard Olga gasp. Running into the living room, Cato saw her mother sink into the couch, a look of horror on her face. Amelie, tears flooding her cheeks, whispered that Professor Lessing had been "discovered" in Marienbad, Czechoslovakia. According to the radio announcer, "unknown assailants" had murdered him.

His death shocked Cato into realizing how relentless the Nazis were in tracking down their enemies. How dangerous it would be to reveal anything said against them, even in jest!

As a twelve-year-old, Cato found it hard to believe that Hitler would last. Surely, Germans would rise up against the Nazis and overthrow them. The wisest thing, she told Mietje, was to ignore them as much as possible, just as she pretended that her parents weren't really divorced.

But then, Jan wrote that he had remarried and wanted everyone to meet his new wife, Rali. Cato was stunned—how could he? And how should she react toward her stepmother? Should she even meet her? Torn by her loyalty to Olga, she asked her mother what to do.

"I told Cato I could never hate anyone, and she shouldn't either. Jan was her father."

When Jan and Rali arrived in Fischerhude, Cato watched from the window as the, auburn-haired young woman got out of the car. To Cato, Rali's high heels, silk stockings, white gloves, and chic black frock represented an elegance seen only in borrowed magazines. Jan, in a yellow silk shirt, looked as well turned out as his new wife. The suitcase he carried was made of the finest leather.

Shyly, Mietje smoothed her faded frock. Cato puffed up her sleeves, and the girls went out to greet them. Tim, furious over Jan's leaving, waited until they came into the house.

With the newlyweds' visit, Cato realized that she could not control or dream away things she wished were otherwise. She had to accept her father's marriage. It was a fact. And she liked Rali, who shared her love of books.

It was also a reality that Hitler controlled the lives of every German. Equally terrifying was to hear her beloved Ulrich praise the Nazis. Though she cringed when he spoke, Cato vowed to do everything she could to change Ulrich's mind.

Chapter 7

Swimming against the Tide

Cato burst into the kitchen. The school master had just announced that a branch of the Hitler Youth was being formed in Fischerhude. Without pausing, Cato recited the activities: hiking, overnight camping trips, track meets between the villages, singing, dramatics . . . *and*, when she was seventeen, she could join the Fliegerkorps (flying club). Through the Hitler Youth, she could learn to fly!

When she did stop for a breath, Cato realized that Amelie and Mama were uncharacteristically silent. Amelie usually blurted out whatever was on her mind, and Olga always had a word of encouragement, no matter how wild Cato's plans. Now they sat there, stunned.

Cato was the best athlete in the school. In the broad jump, discus throwing, and the 100-and-200-yard dashes, she always came in first. Unless Cato joined the Hitler Youth, she would be barred from the competitions between the villages. The Nazis had banned all other sports clubs and youth groups.

While Cato's participation in sports might be harmless, Olga and Amelie knew that the objective of the Hitler Youth was to turn young people into fervent Nazis, young people willing to fight and die for Adolf Hitler. In the Hitler Youth, children were taught they were members of a "master race." As members of the master race, they had the right to rule over "inferior peoples." If parents objected to this philosophy, members of the Hitler Youth had a duty to report them to the authorities.

Taking her mother's silence for approval, Cato gleefully reported that all members of the Hitler Youth were excused from school on Saturdays. Until then, German children attended school six days a week. For Cato, not having to squirm on the school bench one extra day was a godsend. Before Olga could think of how to discourage Cato, a former schoolmate of Olga's knocked on the door.

"As a good friend," the woman told her, "I'm warning you. If you discourage your children from joining the Hitler Youth, there will be serious consequences."

Olga did not answer.

"Surely you are aware," the neighbor said, "that people who continue to oppose the party disappear."

Olga was frightened. She knew about the concentration camps, and she didn't want her children to be without a mother as well as a father. But the stakes were too high.

Somehow, she had to make Cato understand that if she joined, she would no longer be free to think for herself. Cato had just finished reading

Uncle Tom's Cabin, by Harriet Beecher Stowe. The novel dealt with slavery in the United States. In the story, Eliza takes her child and runs away from her master to keep him from selling her son to another slaveholder.

For several nights, Cato had awakened Olga to tell her of the nightmares she had after reading the book. Olga decided to relate Hitler's persecution of the Jews to the treatment of blacks in *Uncle Tom's Cabin*. That evening, she took Cato aside and reminded her that the southerners in *Uncle Tom's Cabin* had said they had a right to persecute black people because they were inferior. "In the Hitler Youth, they want to teach you to think that way about Jews and other people the Nazis don't like. Everything this family has stood for—integrity, honesty, openness—would be destroyed if you joined the Hitler Youth."

Without answering, Cato slipped into the garden. As she climbed to the top branch of the chestnut tree, she looked across the fields. Everything seemed the same—the cows grazing, the dust rising from the horse-drawn hay wagon creaking along the road, and the thin line of smoke drifting across the meadow from the brickyard in Ottersberg. Only it wasn't . . . memories of Theodor's murder . . . having to close the windows when they listened to BBC or when they discussed politics . . . reverting to sign language whenever the children passed a neighbor. . . .

Reluctantly, she admitted Mama was right. Any club with the name Hitler in it was poison.

Cato climbed down from the chestnut tree. In the living room, she told Mietje, Tim, and Maria why she thought they shouldn't join the Hitler Youth.

Mietje didn't mind. "I preferred to spend my free time drawing, rather than marching up and down the road," she relates.

Neither did Tim. He could play stickball with his friends after school, and from the time he first crawled under the piano to watch the movement of the strings, he dreamed of becoming a concert pianist. He needed every extra hour to practice.

As for blond, happy-go-lucky, pigtailed Maria, whatever her cousins wanted to do was fine.

When Cato returned to the kitchen, her bright smile showed Olga, as it always did, that Cato had created her own solution. "Mama, we don't need the Hitler Youth. The four of us can build a track in the meadow and have our own games."

That Saturday, everyone except Cato, Mietje, Tim, Maria, and Albert Wallace was excused from school. Albert's father had been a Social Democrat, and he said his son was "too sickly" to join the Hitler Youth.

As Cato led the "renegades" past the swastika flag flying over the green, she greeted the other children, who were lined up waiting for the arrival of the Hitler Youth leaders. The girls in

A group from the Hitler Youth going off to help harvest crops.

black skirts and white shirts, the boys in black shorts and white shirts, waved back.

Inside the classroom, the Bontjes children could feel the annoyance of the teacher as they slid into their seats on the school bench. "If it weren't for us," Mietje says, "he would have been free to tend his beehives on Saturday."

Herr Heinbuckel glared at Cato. He knew she was the ringleader. "You can't swim against the tide!" he shouted, waving his finger at her.

Cato stood up. "Yes, I can, Herr Heinbuckel. Yes, I can."

CHAPTER 8

The Day They Murdered the Books

The following Monday, Cato sat in the classroom glaring at the picture of Adolf Hitler hanging over the blackboard. She wanted to jump up and tear it into bits.

For the second time, the schoolmaster cleared his throat. Then he said, "The minister of education has asked us to correct some errors in our textbooks, since the village is too poor to buy the new ones issued by the party. Please turn to page seventy-nine."

There was a rustle as everyone leafed through the book.

Cato stared at the picture of Heinrich Heine: "Heinrich Heine, born 1797, died 1856, one of Germany's greatest lyric poets. . . . Poet of the people." Every German composer Cato knew seemed to have put Heine's poems to music. Did that mean they could no longer sing his songs? Heine was born a Jew, but he had converted to Christianity. Blood was blood, according to the Nazis.

"All references to Heine are to be removed." The teacher looked confused. He checked the paper on his desk to make sure he had read it correctly.

One of the boys whooped, "No more memorizing Heine!"

"Quietly," the teacher murmured.

A tear slipped down Cato's cheek, but her hands froze.

"Cato," the schoolmaster said, placing a ruler against the spine of her book.

Cato winced as the sound of page after page being torn from the bindings rippled across the room. Good bye, Heine.

The teacher wet his index finger with his tongue and turned to another section. "Page ninety four," he called, fingering the paper. "Ninety four, five, six, seven, and eight, out." August von Wasserman, Jew, discoverer of test for syphilis, rip out. The ragged edges increased. Thomas Mann, Christian, Nobel Prize winner, hater of Hitler and war . . . tear to bits.

When school ended, Cato stared at her textbook. Only German grammar remained untouched. History, literature, science, art, music—slashed, trashed, hanging by threads.

At last the bell rang. Cato, instead of jumping up and rushing outside, walked slowly through the door. Without a word, Cato, Tim, Maria, and Mietje gathered in the churchyard and made their way around the white tombstones, across the street, and down the dirt path leading toward the house.

Cato glanced over her shoulder to see if the other children were in sight. Her hands shaking, she began to sign, "At least, Emma and Jossi will send us books from Berlin."

Her fingers dropped to her side. "No!" she whispered aloud, recalling the evening of May 10, 1933. That night, Cato had been in the living room dancing to an American song playing on the radio, "I've Got Rhythm." Papa had taught her some tap steps on his last visit, and she was showing Mietje a buck-and-wing.

Abruptly, the music stopped. A news broadcast followed: "Tonight all over Germany, students are ridding our libraries of subversive materials and throwing these ignominious volumes into the bonfires burning in front of universities and libraries."

Someone began to call out the names of the authors whose books were being tossed into the flames in front of the University of Berlin. Cato held her hands over her ears.

"Theodor Lessing, Thomas Mann, Sigmund Freud, Heinrich Heine, Lion Feuchtwanger . . . ." The voice, triumphant, moved on to foreign authors: "Émile Zola, H. G. Wells, Upton Sinclair, Jack London, Pearl Buck, Sinclair Lewis . . . ."

Then the minister of propaganda, Josef Göebbels, took the microphone and proclaimed, "These flames not only illuminate the final end of an old era, they also light up a new one."

Amelie, her arms around her trembling niece, repeated Heine's warning of a hundred years ago, "Those who burn books soon burn people."

Now, a year after the book burnings in the larger cities, Nazi fingers were reaching into the villages to destroy the works of any authors who spoke for freedom. Cato realized that if someone inspected the books on their living room shelves, Mama and Amelie could be arrested.

The four dashed home and burst into Olga's studio. She looked up from the still life she was painting. "What's the matter?"

"We've got to get Heine and Helen Keller off the shelves," Cato said, handing her mother the mutilated textbook.

In a whirlwind, everyone grabbed books and raced up the steps. Only the Bible and a few ancient travel books remained on the living room shelves. To fill in the empty spaces, Olga placed photographs and vases and some of Amelie's sculptures on the shelves.

Despite the threat of discovery, Olga and Amelie vowed the Nazis would not prevent them from teaching the children the values they cherished: the dignity of each individual and an open mind. Amelie, with her knowledge of history, philosophy, and political science, would continue to discuss, inside the house, the works of those authors who had been banned. And to teach them French, though the learning of foreign languages was frowned upon.

But they would have to be careful.

That evening, Cato, Miejte, and Tim closed the windows as Olga played Mendelssohn's "Overture to *A Midsummer Night's Dream*."

Except when Ulrich was present, the family played and discussed whatever they pleased. Though Amelie felt her nephew Ulrich, who had joined the Storm Troopers, would never betray the family, it was best to be careful.

Berlin, May 10, 1933. One of the many book burnings held throughout Germany to destroy books banned by the Nazis.

Heathens

Cato hated the taunts. As soon as she, Mietje, and Tim entered the classroom, their classmates began to snicker, "Heathens! Heathens! Heathens!" The noise grew louder and louder until the schoolmaster rapped his stick.

Since the Bontjes children had never been baptized, they were excused from religious instruction the first period in the morning. Their classmates resented their not having to arrive at the same time.

Cato wasn't sure what a heathen was, but she didn't like being teased. Jan, who was against all religions, forbade Olga to baptize them at birth. Though Olga was a Protestant and played the organ in church, she respected Jan's wishes.

After weeks of being called heathens, Cato asked Olga what a heathen was.

"I told her," Olga says, "that it was anyone who didn't believe in the religion that you practiced."

Cato didn't understand her mother's answer. But she told Meme and Tim they ought to investigate Christianity, since they didn't want to be too different from the others. Amelie told her to read the Bible, especially Matthew in the New Testament. While Cato liked the stories, some of the Bible seemed like fairy tales.

Neither could she understand how the people in the village, all of whom were Christians, never protested the Nazis putting people in concentration camps. That wasn't "loving your neighbor as yourself," she told Olga.

In school, the teacher and students knew the Ten Commandments, but no one said it was dishonest to tear pages out of the textbooks.

Still, Cato wanted to explore Christianity. In 1933, shortly after Hitler came to power, Grossmutter had died. It was still hard for Cato to believe that she would never see her beloved grandmother again. Christianity believed in an afterlife. If this were true, then one day, if she were a Christian, she would see Grossmutter and meet Grossvater.

With all her questions about Christianity, Cato decided to drop in on Pastor Tidow. A surprised minister invited her into his study. With awe, Cato stared at the books on his shelves. Her lips moved silently as she read the names of the authors: Freud, Sinclair Lewis, Helen Keller, Feuchtwangler, Lessing.

For the pastor not to hide the books was an act of courage. Pastor Tidow, seeing her joy in the books, invited Cato to borrow them. He also offered to discuss them with her.

"They developed a special relationship," Olga

recalls. "He loved literature, and he was delighted to have such a bright student." Pastor Tidow was allied with the Confessing Church, a group of Protestant ministers against Hitler, and he saw special qualities in Cato.

Slowly, Cato told Tim and Mietje, she was coming to the conclusion that they *might* consider becoming Christians, even though she had more questions than the pastor could answer.

Amelie, who tried not to interfere, encouraged the children to join the church. She was particularly urgent after the last visit of Heinrich Peper, the local *gauleiter*. Herr Peper, a carpenter by trade, had joined the Nazi party before Hitler came to power. As a reward, he was put in charge of the district (*gau*), which had jurisdiction over the local villages.

The *gauleiter* dropped by from time to time to discuss art with Amelie and Olga. That afternoon, as he sat in the living room sipping a cup of tea, he suggested that since the children were not Christians, they should be baptized as Nazis and "dedicated to Adolf Hitler in a beautiful ceremony in the woods."

Cato, listening in the hallway, ran outside. Peper was a fool. They hadn't joined the Hitler Youth. Why would they want to take an oath to Hitler in a pagan ceremony in front of a tree stump? She'd rather be a Christian than a Nazi. If they were baptized, Cato reasoned, Peper would leave them alone.

After much discussion, Cato, Mietje, and Tim agreed to be baptized, but not in the church. The three carried buckets of water from the Wuemme into the living room. There, under the picture of Heinrich Breling, Pastor Tidow baptized them.

Ordinarily, students were confirmed when they reached fourteen, and Cato's class had been preparing for the ceremony for the past few years. Since Cato had had no previous religious instruction, Pastor Tidow offered to tutor her so she could be confirmed with her peers.

Cato accepted. The pastor's study became a sanctuary, a beacon in an ever-darkening horizon. In a world where most pastors and priests either agreed with Hitler's theories of a master race, or kept silent, she struggled to understand the true meaning of Christianity.

The day of confirmation, Cato, wearing a black dress, entered the white chapel. For centuries, the ritual had not varied. Confirmants were asked questions about what they had learned. Word for word, they responded with memorized passages.

Frequently, the snores of tired farmers echoed through the church as they enjoyed a rare morning's nap. This morning, when Cato stood up to be questioned, the shocked farmers' wives jarred them awake so they could hear the blasphemy—Cato Bontjes van Beek, instead of repeating the answer she was supposed to have memorized, was answering a question with a question!

Mietje remembers Cato's words. "Pastor Tidow," she said, "in Matthew 21, verses 18-21, a hungry Jesus comes upon a fig tree that has only leaves, since it was not the season for it to bear fruit. As punishment for not having any fruit, Jesus causes the tree to wither. Why did Jesus harm the fig tree? It wasn't a very Christian thing to do."

Neither Olga, Mietje, nor Tim recalls the pastor's answer, only the silence.

After church, the parishoners, as they walked down the steps and across the churchyard strewn with ancient gravestones, wondered aloud where this blasphemy would lead. The girl certainly was a problem.

CHAPTER **10**

The Olympics

Cato hated the idea of attending secretarial school. As was the case for most German children, Cato's formal schooling ended at fourteen. Only the academically gifted went on to the gymnasium, or high school. Though Cato knew more about art and literature than most students, she could never have passed the math and science tests. But she didn't care. She dreamed of becoming an actress.

However, there was no money for drama lessons, and she had to find a way of earning a living. Though Jan and Rali agreed to pay her tuition to secretarial school, Cato was not too happy with the idea of spending her life in front of a typewriter. She promised herself that once she began to earn money, she would take acting lessons.

Fortunately, her studies had to be postponed for six months, since Hitler had decreed that every teenager must spend half a year as a mother's helper. As innocent as it seemed, it was part of Hitler's master plan to conquer the world. To fight his future battles, he would need millions of soldiers, and he urged every woman, married or unmarried, to produce babies as her "patriotic duty." To teach these young women housekeeping skills, he ordered them to serve "voluntarily" in homes with young children.

Cato was lucky. Aunt Haina, who lived at the end of the lane, had just had a baby. She taught Cato how to care for little Olga, to cook, to clean, and when the baby was napping, they secretly studied English.

That summer, Cato had a special incentive for wanting to learn the English. Next year, the Olympics would be held in Berlin, and friends of Amelie's were coming from Great Britain to see the events. One young woman, a schoolteacher, planned to stop in Fischerhude.

For Cato, the six months at Haina's ended too quickly. Then it was off to the School of Commerce in Bremen. Though she hated bookkeeping and shorthand, Cato quickly made friends. Like other sports-crazy Germans, the students talked of nothing else but the forthcoming Olympics. Newspapers carried every detail of the magnificent stadium being built in Berlin to hold 100,000 people. Special housing for the contestants, a swimming stadium large enough for 10,000 spectators, broad avenues, housing for the participants, and restaurants made the Olympic village a city within a city.

To Hitler, the Olympics were a chance to flaunt the accomplishments of the Third Reich. Not only did he feel that his blond, blue-eyed Aryan supermen and superwomen would take every medal, but he wanted to show off his superhighway system, the autobahn.

To hide his persecution of Jews from the thousands of visitors pouring into Germany, Hitler ordered the removal of all anti-Jewish signs. One morning, when Cato took the train into Bremen, she noticed that the signs "Jews Enter at Your Own Risk" had been removed from each of the railroad stops leading to the city. When she got off the train and started to walk toward school, she saw that the signs pasted on the fronts of Jewish stores, "Do Not Buy from Jews," had vanished.

Still, a nation trained to hate had difficulty controlling itself. With her special interest in track, Cato read and reread the sports pages the girls shared with her. Silently, she fumed whenever a sportswriter criticized the American teams for including black athletes. But only behind the locked doors of the house, at 38 In Der Bredenau, did she express her anger.

That summer, Cato jumped up and down and clapped when the radio reported that Jesse Owens, a black American, took first place in a track meet. Hitler, who had personally handed out the awards to gold medalists, left the stadium to avoid presenting Owens with his gold medal. Mietje remembers Cato weeping at the insult.

"She simply could not understand Hitler discriminating against a person because of his color," Miejte says. "When Owens took three other gold medals, she jumped up and down shouting with joy."

Despite Cato's anguish over the humiliation of Jesse Owens and other black athletes, the Olympic events did bring a special guest to Fischerhude.

Pat Beesley stepped off the bus carrying a suitcase filled with green dresses and jangling bracelets. The whole village wanted to get a look at the short, slim redhead, especially the farmers'

Jesse Owens, American track star, winner of four gold medals in the 1936 Olympics.

sons. The Gestapo also took note: Amelie Breling was entertaining foreigners from Great Britain.

Though Cato was sixteen and Pat twenty-one, they became instant friends. "She had this big smile," Pat says, "which filled the room."

Despite her warm reception, Pat had an uncomfortable feeling as she and Cato wandered through the village. Outside the house, Cato's usually buoyant voice dropped several decibels. "I had never come across this business before," Pat recalls, "where you couldn't say what you pleased. People seemed to be afraid of one another."

But Pat did not lack for entertainment. Ulrich was now using one of the Brelings' studios to paint, and his friends dropped by to escort Pat and Cato to the tavern for a beer. Like most teenagers, Cato had a lively interest in boys. But she found the young men in the village dull. They never opened a book! Most of them joined the Storm Troopers. On Saturdays, they marched up and down the dusty roads singing Nazi songs. Cato thought they looked silly in their ill-fitting, secondhand uniforms and the ridiculous pillbox-shaped hats held under their chins by a strap.

Discouraged, she asked Pat about English boys: "Do they like to read? Are any of them interested in philosophy?" Cato had discovered the writings of a Chinese philosopher, Lao-Tzu, and like someone seized by a disease, went around quoting him to anyone who would listen. Pat, who had young men on her mind rather than philosophers, told her to come and see for herself.

Cato laughed. It seemed impossible that she would ever have enough money to leave Germany.

Shortly after Pat returned home, her mother wrote to Cato and invited her to spend two months in England as a mother's helper. At a time when refugees were pouring into the country, it was the only way Mrs. Beesley could obtain a visitor's permit for a sixteen-year-old.

Suddenly a new world was opening for Cato. She might actually see the places she had "flown over" in the imaginary flights taken from the cockpit built in the sand: Shakespeare's theater at Stratford-on-Avon, the River Thames, Coventry Cathedral. But where would she get the money for her passage?

Amelie and Olga knew this was an unusual opportunity, perhaps the only opportunity for Cato to escape, even for a short time, from Germany.

They wrote to their sisters and to Jan. Within a few days, checks arrived from Emma and Jossi in Berlin, from Lolo in the Bavarian Alps, and from Jan and Rali.

Cato, the girl who wanted to fly across oceans, was about to realize one portion of her dream—to step aboard an ocean liner and visit England.

PART II
NEW FACES, NEW PLACES

1935-1940

CHAPTER 11

Merry England

In her bobby socks and with a suitcase stuffed full of books on Chinese and Indian mysticism, sixteen-year-old Cato sailed off to England.

Grete-Wynchcombe, the tiny village in which the Beesleys lived, lay among the gently rolling hills of the Cotswolds, not far from Stratford-on-Avon, the birthplace of William Shakespeare. Sheep with black noses and feet dotted the countryside, as they had in Shakespeare's time. Like the house in Fischerhude, the Beesleys' cottage was surrounded by a spacious lawn and fruit trees. But the atmosphere was entirely different.

On Saturdays, young men did not parade up and down the road in Storm Troopers' uniforms. They played cricket or slammed balls over a tennis net. Nor were they concerned about being called up for the armed forces. Unlike Germany, England had no desire to fight another war.

England had lost more than a million men in the World War I, and another war was unthinkable.

To Cato, being able to turn on the shortwave radio without first posting guards at the doors and windows was the biggest thrill. Like a child, she stood transfixed, switching first to Radio Orange, the Dutch station, then to France, to Belgium, to Germany. Göbbel's gutteral voice made her return to the British Broadcasting Corporation.

Imagine! The announcer was criticizing the former king, Edward VIII, for renouncing his throne to marry a commoner, Wallis Simpson. Criticism of royalty did not lead to imprisonment! Imagine!

The first time Cato went shopping in nearby Cheltenham, she swooned in front of the bookstore. So many goodies, she wanted to run inside and swoop them up. Not having the money to buy them didn't matter. Just seeing Karl Marx's *Das Capital* next to a biography of Franklin D. Roosevelt, Johann Wolfgang von Goethe sharing a shelf with Walt Whitman's *Leaves of Grass* and H. G. Wells's *War of the Worlds* made her feel as though a heavenly library had opened and rained books.

Unlike the stores in Bremen, which displayed only books approved by the Nazis, British shop windows offered books of every political viewpoint, including Winston Churchill's *The Gathering Storm*. Churchill, a member of the cabinet, warned of Hitler's plans to drag the world into another war. Most people in England thought Churchill's ideas were farfetched, despite pictures in the *"The London Illustrated"* magazine of German tanks and planes.

Mr. Beesley was among the few who agreed with Churchill. In front of friends and strangers, he criticized the government for its blindness and argued that the country should be building munitions factories in preparation for the war that was sure to come.

Whenever she heard Mr. Beesley speak, Cato thought she was back in Fischerhude, before Hitler. Enthralled, she listened as hard as she could.

But although she had a gift for languages and tried to remember the idioms, she sometimes got things mixed up. Pat remembers her saying, "Clock nine I go to bed and clock nine I get up."

"And that's what she did," Pat adds, "unless it was a party night. She was a serious and thoughtful girl but one with a great sense of fun."

And part of the fun was meeting a young agricultural student, John Hall. One day, Muriel Beesley gave a "coffee" to introduce Cato to the local ladies. Never at a loss for conversation, even when she wasn't fluent in a language, Cato told John's grandmother of her interest in Chinese and Indian mystics. Mrs. Hall hugged her. For months, her grandson had been trying to find someone with whom he could discuss Chinese philosophers. John's grandmother immediately invited Cato to tea.

John was the first boy Cato really liked. Slim,

ginger-haired, and over six feet tall, the handsome young man not only talked about mysticism but also quoted the romantic poetry of Percy Bysshe Shelley. He was studying agriculture at the local college, and sometimes he borrowed his parents' Rover, a car with an open top, to take Cato to a movie. More often, they rode bicycles to the tennis courts or walked to dances held in a local hall.

On weekends, the Beesleys liked to take Cato sightseeing—to nearby Warwickshire Castle, to Stratford-on-Avon so she could wander along the narrow cobblestone streets, and to the cathedral in Coventry. But her favorite Sunday morning activity was going out to the flying field on the way to Oxford and watching gliders being lifted into the air.

Cato not only loved the freedom she had in England, but as her feelings for John became more than a schoolgirl crush, she asked the Beesleys if it were possible for her to stay longer. Pat and her parents loved Cato's gaiety and spontaniety, and they promised to do everything they could to keep her there. But it was difficult. Refugees, fleeing for their lives, had priority.

At a meeting with an "influential" person, Cato learned that there was not much hope of having her visa extended, since the British Foreign Office judged Cato "in no danger" from the Nazi regime. In March, shortly before she was to leave, Cato wrote to her friend Annita that she was "quite depressed." But she also mentioned, "I dreamed I had boarded the ship in Southampton, but on the ship I still had hope that the Home Office would give me permission to stay."

In the past, many of Cato's dreams had come true, and with her usual optimism, she refused to be completely discouraged.

She dreaded going back to Germany, not only because she felt John was *the* man in her life, and she needed more time to be sure, but because she hated the thought of having to revert to sign language to say whatever she pleased.

At this point, all she could do was hope her dream would come true, and at the last minute, the British Foreign Office would extend her visa.

Chapter 12

Another Chance

C ato let out a whoop. It was just like her dream! Two hours before she was to leave for Southampton to board the ship, the mailman handed her a letter. It was from the British Home Office. "Miss Bontjes van Beek's visa is hereby extended for another six months." Cato immediately went to the phone and called John's grandmother.

As she did the dishes that evening, she recited Shelley's poem over and over, "Oh, to be in England, now that spring is here . . ."

With the warm weather, Cato and John began to spend more time outdoors. On weekends, they drove his grandfather's trap, a small two-wheeled wagon drawn by a pony, to the top of Cleve Hill for midnight picnics. As they joined Pat and other friends around the campfire, they roasted potatoes and sausages and sang.

Pat remembers Cato's lovely voice. "At first she sang in German, and nobody knew what she was singing. Then she quickly picked up our songs."

Though he was free on weekends, John was a student at the agricultural school and had to study during the week. Cato, too, had obligations. She had come to England as a mother's helper. With the blossoming of purple and yellow crocuses, English housewifes turned their houses upside down in a frenzy of spring cleaning: a rite unheard of in Fischerhude. In the flurry of washing windows, dusting pictures, and cleaning slipcovers, Cato wrote to Annita, "one doesn't know where one can sit down." But once the mops and buckets returned to the closet, Cato could spend more time with John.

By July, Cato and John were certain they were in love. "When we were alone," John says, "we went to Greet Woods to listen to the nightingales. It's an extensive, lovely wood that shelters the whole valley." It was here that John sat beneath a tree and read aloud hour after hour their favorite poems by Shelley.

Cato was so much in love with the handsome redhead that she tried to have her visa extended a second time. The Beesleys appealed to the Home Office. The Home Office was firm. Cato was a minor and could not apply for a work permit. She had to return to Germany on August 8.

No one was more miserable about her departure than John. He was sure he wanted to marry her, and under their favorite tree, he proposed. A very happy Cato said yes, though she knew their engagement would be a long one. Before John could take on the responsibilities of a wife, he had to repay his father for his education. The

Beesleys, who liked John very much, were re-
lieved Cato would return to England.

Because she was so crazy about flying, Mr.
Beesley decided to treat Cato to her first plane
ride. To this day, Pat recalls the event with
horror:

> My mother considered flying
> dangerous, and she said she had to
> write to Amelie and Olga for
> permission for Cato to fly. Amelie
> wrote back, "Cato can do anything
> provided Pat does it, too."

> So I got lumped in. I hate planes.
> Always have, always will. But I said,
> "OK." She was so keen to go. So we
> go up in this little gray monoplane,
> the wings and this cockpit, and you're
> strapped in sort of open to the air.
> There's no cabin.

> We had a fly around. We came
> down, and that was all right. We
> came down!

> Then Cato said, "Now we loop the
> loop!"

> And then the pilot did just that. It's
> a horrible thing. The plane shoots
> straight up into the sky and then into
> a dive. Then straight up and back
> into another dive. When we were at
> the top of the loop, I was terrified I

would fall out. And at the bottom of the loop, I was squashed into the seat with my breath squeezed out of me.

Finally, we landed!

And then Cato said, "And now we do a parachute jump."

I turned green.

Then the pilot asked, "How old are you, young lady?"

"I am sixteen," she said authoritatively.

He said, "We can't let you jump until you're eighteen."

And was I thankful!

Just before Cato left, John gave her a volume of Shelley's poems. On the frontispiece, he copied one of the verses:

I am the daughter of earth and water . . .

And the nursling of the sky

I change

But I cannot die.

The parting was not as painful as Cato had imagined. John promised to come to Germany in two weeks to meet Mama, Amelie, Mietje, and Tim.

For Mrs. Beesley, Cato's departure was a catastrophe. She was sure there was going to be a war. If there were, Cato might never return. As they said good bye, Mrs. Beesley promised to do everything she could to bring not only Cato but Meme and Tim to England.

As the ship slid out to sea, Cato shouted from the top deck, *"Hals und beinbruch!"* "Break a leg!" is an expression theater people use to wish one another luck. With her usual exuberance, Cato added the word <u>neck</u> to the phrase.

That night, as she lay in a lounge chair watching the stars, she knew she had always been lucky. Surely Mrs. Beesley would be successful in bringing her back to England and John. Gazing at the Big Dipper and the North Star, she refused to think of the alternative.

Chapter 13

A Summons from the Gestapo

In Bremen, Cato bounced down the gang plank eager to tell everyone about John. But before she could go through customs, an official grabbed her by the arm and led her into a cubicle.

"Strip," the woman said.

Cato shivered as she stood there naked. Unable to express her indignation, she pursed her lips to keep from screaming as the woman's fingers twisted each lock of Cato's hair. Then she inspected Cato's ears, her nose, her mouth, as if she were a diseased animal, and in the final humiliation ran her fingers across every opening in Cato's body. When she found no secret messages or diamonds, the inspector barked, "Get dressed."

Too angry and stunned to move quickly, Cato reached for her underwear and socks. An involuntary "Oh" escaped from her lips as she saw her skirts and blouses, her photographs of fliers, scattered across the floor as the guard tossed them aside to search the lining of Cato's suitcase.

The woman held up the book of poems John had given Cato. "A book in a foreign language!

It's forbidden."

"It's only poems," Cato said hoarsely, her eyes pleading with the woman. "From my boyfriend."

The inspector frowned. Shrugging her shoulders, she stamped a paper and waved Cato through.

Trembling, Cato entered the waiting room. As she looked around, she saw Mama and Haina standing next to the exit. Instead of rushing forward, they motioned for her to come to them. Despite their smiles, they appeared frightened. With quick hugs, they led Cato outside.

"When they went to the receiving room," Mietje says, "the guard checked their names against the list of incoming passengers. Because there was a black mark next to Cato's name, Mama and Haina were taken into separate rooms and told to undress. The guard strip-searched them."

As they rode the trolley to the railroad station, Cato saw that Germany had not changed. The trolley had to stop while Storm Troopers paraded, singing, across the street.

It was with great relief that they reached home. Inside the house, Cato began to talk nonstop about John and England. As she dug into the plum and noodle pudding Mama had prepared, Cato amused everyone with imitations of her English friends. That evening, Aunt Haina played the violin, and Tim and Mama performed a Bach duet. Cato danced around the living room imitating the British musical comedy star Beatrice Lillie.

After everyone else had gone to bed, Cato and Mietje stayed up late talking of John and of Cato's plans to return to England. The next day, Mietje helped Cato tack her collection of fliers' and actors' photos above the wall behind Cato's bed.

For a few days, Cato drifted lazily down the Wuemme, enjoying the late summer weather. But a call from the police to report to the station cut short her reveries. Cato wondered why she had been summoned. She had done nothing wrong. Was it something to do with the family? Mietje had told her that while she was in England, their father had sent a "Syrian" and his pregnant wife to stay with Amelie and Olga. Mr. and Mrs. Abu, who were in fact Jewish, needed a hiding place until their visas arrived. It was possible that someone had reported Olga and Amelie to the police, and the officers wanted to question Cato.

To her surprise, it was not the local police but the Gestapo who awaited her at the station-house. "They wanted to know what she had done in England, and they asked her if she had visited any airfields," Mietje recalls. "She told them she was a maid. She had seen nothing. The idea that she was supposed to spy on her friends angered Cato."

Since they were unable to obtain any information, the Gestapo let her go.

That week, the postman came up the path with a letter from John. With great excitement, she ran into the studio to tell Mama and Amelie that he had booked passage for the end of August. Cato could hardly wait for the family to meet him. She was certain Mama, Mietje, and Tim, and all her aunts and uncles would adore him.

When his ship docked, John took the bus from Bremen to Fischerhude. Everyone standing in the square gawked as the handsome redhead stepped off the bus. Not only did John tower over most of the villagers, but he was wearing a navy blazer. "In Fischerhude, no one had ever seen a blazer," Annita says. "Obviously, he was a British spy!"

Someone contacted the Gestapo. If a foreigner came to see Cato, she must be a spy, too. Cato had the feeling, as she and John wandered through the woods or paused to sit beneath a birch tree to read poetry, that they were being shadowed. It was only when they took the train to Bremen to see a movie or to visit friends that she felt free from surveillance.

After spending two weeks in Fischerhude, John was anxious for Cato to join him in England. "This business of having to lock the doors every time they played Bloch or Mendelssohn was appalling," he says. And there was the constant fear that Fritz Schmidt might be arrested because he had been a member of the Social Democratic party."

John left, promising to return the following summer. Neither he nor Cato considered the possibility that she might be prevented from returning to England.

A few weeks later, Cato received a letter from her father and Rali inviting her to study in Berlin. The Lette Schule, where they planned to enroll her, was a combination secretarial and "finishing" school. There she would sharpen her shorthand, bookkeeping, and typing skills, and learn manners and how to dress. Jan felt his country-bred daughter needed a little polish. To Cato's delight, Rali added a postscript, "We look forward to taking you to cabarets and to the theater."

Cato's dream of becoming an actress had not vanished. In the theaters of Berlin, she could study the techniques of Germany's finest actors and actresses. Once she completed her course and got a job, she would have enough money for drama lessons.

As she packed her bags, she realized that another dream could come true—to fly. Since the Hitler Youth was now compulsory, she would join the Fliegerkorps, the glider club. Like Amelia Earhart, Cato Bontjes van Beek would touch the stars.

Chapter 14

The Shattered Glass

"My God, she looks like a peasant," Jan said as the train from Bremen rolled into Berlin.

Cato was standing at the door waiting for the car to stop. Her blond hair was twisted around her head and pinned into a bun, and she was wearing heavy wool kneesocks. In one hand she gripped a cardboard suitcase, and in the other, a basket of eggs.

"Take her shopping, immediately," Jan told Rali as they moved forward to greet a beaming Cato.

That night, Jan wrote to Olga, since she was too poor to afford a telephone, "Tell her to cut her hair so she won't look like a farmer's daughter."

The following morning, Rali and Cato set out for the Kurfürstendamm, Berlin's most fashionable street. Cato held her breath as Rali ushered her into a shop displaying cashmere sweaters in every color. As she tried one on with a Scottish plaid skirt, Cato did a Highland fling.

The salesgirl fluttering over them brought out one dress after another until Rali selected two that minimized Cato's broad shoulders and flattered her figure.

Their arms loaded with boxes, and Cato's first pairs of silk stockings, Rali led Cato to Kranzlers. Sitting at an outdoor table, they ordered coffee and strudel. The pastry arrived oozing with apples and raisins. Men passing by stopped for a second glance at Rali, and then, seeing Cato's radiant face, tipped their hats to both of them.

Since Jan and Rali had three small children, their apartment was not large enough for permanent guests. Instead, Cato shared a room with her cousin, Marianne, at the home of Cato's Aunt Jossi and Uncle Hans Schultze-Ritter in Charlottenburg. Another aunt, Emma Breling, lived with the Schultze-Ritters. Stroopi, a schnauzer puppy, completed the household.

Cato felt very much at home. Jossi was a composer, and Hans, a conductor. Marianne, who played the cello and the recorder, was a student at the conservatory. Berlin's most famous musicians often popped in to join their nightly concerts.

Charlottenburg was close to the Tiergarten, the zoo, with its parks and outdoor cafés. On the Kurfürstendam, Berlin's most fashionable avenue, the Café Leon sported a room with a retractable roof for dancing "under the stars," weather permitting. At Alexanderplatz, the Femina Café had telephones on each table to permit guests to send and receive messages. As soon as Cato sat down, the phone began to ring with invitations to dance.

With a broad smile, Cato nodded. Medical students, young soldiers on leave, and junior officials at the Foreign Ministry vied with one another to take her boating on the Wannsee or to the music halls.

In winter, the cousins and their escorts skated on the nearby lakes or visited museums. For Cato, the city was paradise.

Secretarial school? *"Ach!"* she wrote to Annita. "Stenography gives me a headache . . . Curses! I have the opinion that the dear God created bookkeeping in anger." But Cato knew her studies had to be endured for the sake of more glamorous activities.

Most importantly, she was learning to fly. "Tomorrow evening, we are building an airplane [glider] again, and I know how to plane the wood and glue up the parts. It gives me much pleasure." Since the Hitler Youth was now compulsory, Cato had joined the Fliegerkorps. As member no. 540066, she jumped out of bed every Sunday morning at five to attend the meetings. She also enjoyed the camaraderie of the other young women. Most of them greeted her with *"Guten Tag,"* rather than the Nazi salute and *"Heil Hitler."*

Though Cato was enormously busy, she wrote to John every day. His letters, filled with poetry and declarations of love, flowed across the ocean. While she enjoyed the company of other young men, Cato dreamed of returning to England and marrying John. In her last letter, Mrs.

Beesley wrote that she had arranged for Cato to become an apprentice to an English potter. The man, Michael Cardew, had written to the British Home Office requesting a visa for Cato.

But on March 12, the opening bars of Beethoven's "Fifth Symphony" sounded on the radio, signaling a momentous event. German troops had marched into Austria. Later, at the movies, Cato saw newsreels of Austrians dancing in the streets to welcome their conquerors. Other scenes revealed German soldiers forcing Jewish men and women to get down on their hands and knees and scrub the sidewalks of Vienna. While most Berliners in the theater stood up and cheered, Cato walked out, repulsed and afraid. Unless her visa arrived soon, she might never escape from a country that had lost all sense of human dignity.

Despite the social whirl and the fun of the Fliegerkorps, it was a relief, that summer, to finish her course and return to the fields of Fischerhude. Though John's visit in August was short, it was long enough to reaffirm their feelings. John had spoken to Michael Cardew, the potter, and Michael felt confident the Home Office would issue Cato a visa.

By late September, when the visa had not come, Cato began work as a secretary in Bremen for an electrical firm, Heyse und Escherbuerg. She and Mietje took the train to Bremen each day, passing the belching smokestacks of factories turning out munitions.

Her sense of onrushing disaster intensified in late September when Hitler demanded that Czechoslovakia cede the western part of its country, the Sudetenland, to Germany. The prime minister of Britain and the prime minister of France flew to Munich to talk with Hitler. In return for Hitler agreeing to "no further territorial demands," they permitted him to march into Czechoslovakia. Unlike the Austrians, who had danced in the streets to welcome Hitler, the Czechs cried. In Cato's house, it was a day of mourning.

The Nazi menace soon struck closer to home. On the afternoon of November 9, Olga was summoned to a neighbor's phone. "It was Kurt Hinterlach, from Berlin," Olga recounts. "He said he had a friend who needed a place to stay, temporarily. Could I accommodate him? I said yes, surmising the friend was Jewish."

The following morning, in Bremen, Cato and Meme discovered why it had been necessary to hide the stranger. As they walked toward the business district, they stopped in shock before a smouldering synagogue, unable to believe that someone would set it on fire or that firemen could not save it. Nearby, the windows of Jewish-owned stores were smashed, and shards of glass littered the streets.

Ahead of them, Mietje noticed a crowd of people being herded by a Storm Trooper toward the railroad station. Doris, one of her classmates, was among them. "Doris," she called,

Magdeburg: One of the seventy-six synagogues set on fire throughout Germany on Crystal Night, November 9-10, 1938.

"Hallo! Wait." Doris did not look back. When Mietje glanced at the synagogue, she remembered that Doris was Jewish.

The Nazis claimed this nationwide riot against the Jews was a "spontaneous action." They said the German people were protesting the shooting of a German diplomat in Paris by a Jewish student. There, Herschel Grynzpan had shot the official to avenge the Nazis' deportation of his Polish-born parents. Along with other Polish-born Jews, the Grynzpans were taken to a tiny strip of no-man's-land between Germany and Poland and abandoned without food, water, or shelter.

Using the death of the diplomat as an excuse, the Nazis instigated this nationwide riot against the Jews. From a previously prepared list, Storm Troopers rounded up 30,000 Jewish men and

Crystal Night, November 9-10, 1938. The shattered windows of a Jewish-owned shop.

interned them in concentration camps. Seventy-six synagogues were destroyed, as well as thousands of Jewish homes and businesses.

This night of rioting and looting, with its residue of broken glass, became known as Kristalnacht, Crystal Night.

Cato prayed her visa would arrive before she had to witness further horrors.

CHAPTER 15

The Dream

This time, Cato stopped in the middle of her typing. Usually, she paid no attention to the propaganda spouting over the radio. But the roll of drums, the blast of trumpets, and the opening bars of Beethoven's "Fifth" signaled an important announcement.

Göbbels, the minister of propaganda, came on the air: "At the invitation of the Czech people, German troops have marched into Prague. . . . Our beloved Führer is simply following the wishes of the Czech people to end their oppressive government."

Cato closed her eyes, bidding herself not to scream, "It's a lie!" She knew Czechoslovakia had been a democracy, and after the Sudetenland, Hitler had promised not to seize the rest of Czechoslovakia. As the other girls jumped up and cheered, Cato slipped into the ladies' room and wept.

The next morning, when Cato came into the kitchen for coffee, she said she had had a very frightening dream. As Mietje recalls, "Her face was covered with red blotches from too much weeping. In her eyes, there was fear, sadness, confusion."

The dream was so overwhelming that Cato recorded it in her diary:

March 1939

I had a strange dream. I dreamed that I was sentenced to death together with several others . . . Why, and which crime I had committed, I do not know. After the verdict . . . we were immediately led to the place of execution. On the way we passed through a large hall that was hung with red imitation Persian carpets. In front went the executioner, then the judges, then we convicts, followed by a large crowd of people . . . I knew for sure this was my last walk, but I didn't feel any sorrow. . . .

Suddenly I noticed some agitation among the other convicted persons. . . .

It became clear to me . . . that my fellow prisoners wanted to run away. But I am angry about this and I call them cowards . . . They succeed . . . I am alone.

Remarkably neither the executioner nor the judge nor the crowd have observed the flight. We find ourselves in a long room. I am being shown to a chair . . . which resembles those used by dentists, even the practical headrest . . . I sit down, completely at ease and composed.

Suddenly a march is blasting from a portable gramophone . . . In front of me stands the executioner. Suddenly he is transformed—into Ulrich!

My God, Ulrich is the executioner. . . .

I take a last deep breath and then put my head down onto the headrest—

Then Ulrich may carry out his duty. . . .

CHAPTER 16

A Miracle?

Cato was frightened. If her visa did not come soon, she would be trapped in Germany. Each day, the headlines in the newspapers accused the Polish people of new atrocities: raping of German women, plundering German stores, seizing German farms in the east. According to the propaganda spewing from the radio, Poland intended to invade Germany.

To Amelie, Hitler's strategy was obvious. To justify an attack on Poland, he wanted to convince the Germans that the Poles were the aggressors.

Just when she had given up all hope of leaving, Cato received a note from Michael Cardew, the English potter. In response to his request for a visa for Cato, the British Home Office replied, "Miss van Beek's proper course is to apply for a visa at the nearest British Passport Control Office or Consul."

Cato let out a whoop—that meant Bremen! The next day, she spent her lunch hour at the office of the British consul and received her visa. A short time later, visa in hand, she applied for an exit permit. It came within a few days.

That morning, Cato took an early train to Bremen. The steamship office was jammed with people trying to escape from Germany, and disappointingly, she could not obtain passage until the middle of August.

The day before she was to leave, Cato, stuffing her suitcase full of books, sang, "Summer is a' cummin, gladly sing cuckoo." It was the Shakespearean sonnet she, John, and Pat used to sing on Cleve Hill as they roasted sausages. When she could cram no more books into her suitcase, she called for Mietje's help. The two sat on it until it closed.

That evening, as the girls were finishing the dishes, they heard Tim play the aria from Bach's "Goldberg Variations." Olga stood at the door to the living room, tinkling the small brass bell that through the years had called them to special celebrations. Mietje took Cato by the arm and led her inside.

Amelie, Haina and Fritz, little Olga and Maria, Aennee and Annita, and the Otterstedts applauded as they entered. As the guest of honor, Cato was seated in the center of the couch. The concert began. Aunt Haina started with Bruch's "Concerto in G Minor" for the violin. Tim followed with two Chopin mazurkas, and Olga played Debussy's "Afternoon of the Faun." The evening ended with the girls dancing the tarantella, which Olga had taught them long ago.

Later, in their room, there were tears. Cato and Mietje knew war was imminent. It might be a long time before they would see each other again. Cato, who was caught between the sadness of leaving and her excitement over seeing John, reminded Mietje that Mrs. Beesley was trying to arrange for Mietje and Tim and Annita to follow.

Cato awakened the next morning before dawn and ran outside to pluck a handful of raspberries. Then she climbed the chestnut tree, to get a last look from her favorite perch of the fields and rivers of Fischerhude.

When Olga called her for breakfast, Cato climbed down and went into the kitchen. As they ate their jam and bread, Olga tried to be cheerful, but she had difficulty clearing her throat.

Annita knocked at the door to say a final good-bye, and Cato ran to open it. As the girls stood there, the postman came up the path. He handed Cato a letter. She tore it open, thinking it was from John. Cato let out a wail.

Her exit permit had been canceled!

Chapter 17

War

Two weeks later, Cato thought she was having another nightmare–air raid sirens sounded, church bells pealed, and someone banged on the door. Cato and Meme jumped out of bed and dashed downstairs.

It was Mr. Mueller, the mayor. "The war has started. We've gone into Poland."

Mama and Amelie ran into the living room and turned on the radio. Göbbels was speaking. He said the Polish army had invaded Germany, and Hitler had "no alternative but to attack."

The family stood there, stupefied, as in a series of rapid-fire announcements Göbbels boasted of Germany's nonstop conquest of village after village in western Poland. German Panzer tanks, in a blitzkrieg, a lightning-like sweep, caught the Polish nation unawares. The German air force, the Luftwaffe, Göbbels boasted, bombed Polish radio stations, preventing the government from notifying the Polish people of the invasion.

German Stuka bombers, their sirens roaring, swooped down on the unsuspecting Polish air base and destroyed the planes on the ground. As a flier, Cato could imagine the terrifying roar of the bombers, whose wings had been designed to emit a horrifying noise to frighten the enemy.

Listening to the detailed reports of the German sweep through Poland, Cato wept. Her dream of marrying John and living in tranquil England seemed impossible. As she stood in front of the radio, she prayed that Britain and France would send troops to Poland's rescue. Yet if they did, the two men she loved the most, John and Ulrich, would be fighting against each other. Ulrich's words, uttered not too many years ago in this very living room—"I don't want to die in bed, I want to die on the battlefield fighting for Hitler"—had been fervent.

The British and the French condemned the German attack and warned Hitler that if Germany did not withdraw, they would declare war on Germany.

Hitler ignored the warning, and on September 3, Britain and France declared war. On September 4, the English sent Royal Air Force fighters to bomb nearby Wilhelmshaven and Bremerhaven. The Germans cheered when a British pilot was shot down over Wilhelmshaven.

But the few air attacks on Germany could not stop the assault on Poland. Overpowered by the German war machine, Poland surrendered on September 18.

In Fischerhude, in Bremen, and throughout the country, men and women toasted "our glorious victory" and praised Hitler's leadership.

Germany's national honor had been restored, and newsreels proudly displayed Panzer tanks and infantrymen sweeping across the Polish countryside.

Jan, who had been called up for service in a reserve unit, was released from the army. To celebrate, Jan brought Rali and their three young children to Fischerhude. There was a dual purpose to his visit. He felt he might be called up again, and if so, he wanted to ensure the continuance of his workshop. Would Cato consider coming to Berlin to learn how to manage his business?

Even as children, Cato, Mietje, and Tim had helped in the Fischerhude workshop. They knew how to paint, glaze, and fire the figures and vases. Though she did not plan to make a career as a ceramicist, Cato wanted to help her father. She loved the excitement of Berlin, and if she worked for her father, she would be exempted from service in a defense plant. Air Marshal Hermann Göring had given top priority to the completion of the giant eagle Jan was creating for Göring's Air Ministry. Anyone who worked in the shop was excused from defense work until the eagle was finished. There were also many other orders to be filled.

Because of the quality of Jan's work and his congeniality, Jan had received commissions from Minister of Propaganda Josef Göbbels, as well as other Nazi officials.

With the hope that Britain's and France's entry into the war would shorten the conflict and she would soon be free to marry John, Cato returned to Berlin.

Chapter 18

Hannes

Of all the young people Cato met on her return to Berlin, Hannes Lange was the most unusual. She could tell immediately by his appearance that he was against the Nazis. At a time when the Nazi regime emphasized conformity in everything, including dress, Hannes, a medical student, had a style all his own.

Extremely tall, Hannes always wore an oversize floppy French beret. As he walked through the streets in his gray-green raincoat, he carried an umbrella. In Germany, it was considered unmanly to carry an umbrella, but Hannes delighted in being outlandish and tied a wide pink ribbon in a bow under the handle. Though he came from a wealthy family, he refused to have the hole in the top of his shoe mended.

Hannes was fascinated by Cato. Soon, he was telling Cato that she might never see John again, and she would be wise to marry Hannes. Cato laughed, and told him she would remain faithful to John. Undaunted, Hannes brought his medical books to the workshop and studied as Cato stayed up all night to watch the kilns.

Despite the fun of attending cabarets on weekends with Hannes and seeing her favorite actors and actresses perform on stage, Cato could not shake off her despair. For months, the Germans had occupied Poland, but the British did nothing except bomb ports in northern Germany. Sometimes, these bombs went astray and fell on Fischerhude, and Cato feared that the British dropping of a few bombs would not prevent Hitler from seizing other countries.

On April 9, Cato trembled as she turned on the radio and heard that Germany had attacked Norway and Denmark. Denmark fell rapidly, but the Norwegians, aided by Polish, French, and British units, fought for weeks before being overwhelmed. For Cato, there was the fear that John might be among the troops battling the German army.

Like other young people, Cato was about to be called up for the Arbeitsdienst, or National Labor Service. This involved six months of "voluntary" work on a farm or in a factory. She hated the idea of leaving Berlin or of helping the war effort in any way.

She raged to Jan about having to spend six months with strangers. Surely, the other girls would be members of the Hitler Youth, with their constant "Heil Hitlers." At least in Berlin, she had a circle of anti-Nazi friends, and she could say whatever she pleased. In the Arbeitsdienst, she would have to be silent, a difficult task for Cato under any circumstances.

Originally, Cato was to report for the Arbeitsdienst on April 9, but her service was postponed until the twenty-seventh. Every train was needed to transport troops to Denmark and Norway.

After Denmark's surrender, Germany's citizens became ecstatic. Strangers pounded one another on the back, praising "Adolf, our glorious leader." Toasting the victory in taverns and cabarets, they stuffed themselves with cheese stolen from Denmark and gobbled up beef confiscated from hungry Poles.

A few days before Cato was to leave for East Prussia, she was in the workshop, trying to finish as many ceramic pieces as possible. Jan expected to be called back into the army, and with both of them away, they would be shorthanded. Just as Cato put some vases into the oven to fire, she heard the air raid alarm. She decided to ignore it. For months, there had been one practice drill after another, and everyone felt that the English fliers could not possibly penetrate Berlin's anti-aircraft defenses.

Abruptly, the military march on the radio stopped. "Attention, attention!" the announcer shouted, his voice filled with panic. "This is not a test. Repeat, this is not a test. British bombers are approaching Berlin. Everyone take shelter."

Berlin skyline during an Allied air raid.

Jan, Cato, and the others fled down the steps to safety. As the heavy door swung shut, Cato saw fear and anger on the faces of Berliners. How dare the British strike back?

The ground began to shake as bombs struck nearby buildings. Amid the wails of babies, a teenager fingered her rosary and prayed. People huddled together.

When the "all clear" sounded, the door of the shelter slowly swung open. Carefully stepping around bricks and glass scattered across the steps, Cato choked as she and Jan picked their way through smoke-filled streets. Several nearby buildings had been hit. Was the studio still standing?

People coming out of the shelter began to claw at the stones, searching among the rubble for family and friends. Until then, war was something that happened elsewhere. Now it was devastating Germany.

Berlin after an Allied air raid.

CHAPTER 19

The National Labor Service

With misgivings, Cato left Berlin to fulfill her service in the Arbeitsdienst. As the train taking her to East Prussia chugged across the flat countryside, she wanted to hold her ears. The other eighteen-year-olds serving with her chattered constantly about boys and makeup. Nauseated by their conversation, Cato wanted to flee into the lavatory, lock herself inside, and read a book.

Since most of the girls came from working-class families and did not have much education, they spoke local dialects, rather than the high German, or *hoch Deutch,* that Cato was accustomed to hearing at home and among her friends.

Though she was pleasant, she was frustrated by her inability to hold an intelligent discussion. More than that, the girls had been members of the Hitler Youth, and every time someone mentioned his name, they swooned.

At the farm to which she was assigned, Cato was always cheerful and never complained about helping to plant the potatoes and weed the fields. But her emotional isolation overwhelmed her, particularly on May 10, when Germany seized the Netherlands. For Cato, it was as though she personally had been assaulted. She was half Dutch, and Holland was not just a country in a geography book. As a child, she had visited Jan's sister in Amsterdam, wandering over the bridges and along the canals, enjoying the freedom of the city.

It was an abnormally hot spring, and the girls sweltered in their regulation wool socks and heavy black boots issued by the labor corps. Fortunately, Amelie sent Cato a pair of sandals to wear during the summer. Cato "hung them like flowers on a tree" when she went barefoot after doing her chores.

On May 28, Cato froze when she heard the roll of drums, the blast of trumpets, and the opening bars of Beethoven's "Fifth Symphony." She hated the Nazis using her beloved Beethoven to announce each military action. This time, Minister of Propaganda Göbbels boasted of a major offensive launched against the Allied forces. German troops were advancing toward Dunkirk, a French port just across the border from Belgium. The plan was to entrap the Allied units in Belgium and northern France and keep them from withdrawing into France. If successful, the Germans would capture the British and French forces and end the war.

Within weeks, the Germans succeeded in surrounding the Allied armies in Dunkirk. Off-shore, the German navy aimed its guns at the port to prevent attempts to evacuate the Allied troops by sea.

The French and British mobilized every type of vessel, from destroyers to rowboats, to run the blockade. In a heroic rescue, 350,000 soldiers were evacuated across the channel to England.

But France was now defenseless. On June 22, it surrendered. Only England remained for Germany to conquer.

When they heard the news of France's surrender, the other girls jumped on the tables and cheered. Cato rushed outside and put her head between her knees to keep from fainting. Then she felt Helga's hand on her shoulder.

Helga was the only girl in whom she could confide. Cato not only helped the young woman, who came from a working-class family, with her grammar but suggested books for her to read. Cato wrote about their relationship to her Aunt Lolo, emphazing they were "united in our viewpoints."

Despite Helga's friendship, Cato hated having to serve in the labor corps. When she received a letter from her father saying he expected to be called up for military service, Cato wrote to the head of the Arbeitsdienst asking for an early release. She stated that Reichsmarshal Göring had commissioned a giant eagle, and in the absence of her father, her supervision was necessary.

Cato's appeal was rejected. Instead, her father's induction was postponed. The eagle, according to Reichsmarshal Göring, needed the personal supervision of Jan Bontjes van Beek.

But one day, as she was pulling weeds, an excruciating pain in her leg made her crumple to the ground. The young woman in charge of the Arbeitsdienst helped Cato to the bunkhouse and told her to stay in bed until the pain went away. After a week of inactivity, the pain did not subside. When a doctor examined her, he diagnosed a blood clot and sent her to a hospital. Despite the pain, it was an opportunity for Cato to read once more her dog-eared copy of *Crime and Punishment* and to think about the terrible things the Nazis were doing to Germany and to occupied Europe.

After her leg healed, Cato was released from the Arbeitsdienst since she could no longer work on a farm. As the train sped toward Berlin, Cato vowed to oppose the Nazis. But how?

PART III
FLYING AGAINST THE WIND

1940-1943

CHAPTER 20

A New Awakening

Hannes was waiting for her at the station.
As he handed her a bouquet of chrysan-
themums, he asked her to marry him.
Gently, she reminded him that she was in love
with John. Though Cato knew she might never
see John again, she refused to dwell on it. She
had more immediate concerns.

During her illness, Cato had had a great deal of
time to think about the Nazis and how they were
destroying Germany. As a child, she had told her
mother, "Grown-ups talk. Children must act."
Now, at eighteen, she realized that she had to
take some action. But how? Even making a
joke about Hitler could lead to a death warrant.
What could she, one individual, a teenager, do to
combat the Nazis?

Her question was answered the next morning.
Meme was now studying art in Berlin. As the
two girls waited for the subway, Cato was
startled to see groups of men, in ragged French
uniforms, being shoved into the last car. "Who
are they? And why are people going out of their
way to spit on them?" Cato asked.

"I told her they were prisoners of war who had

been captured when France surrendered in June. The S.S. shipped them in boxcars to Germany," Meme says. "Every day the guards transported them from their primitive housing on the outskirts of Berlin to defense plants where they're used as slave laborers."

Slave labor? Cato couldn't believe such a thing existed in Germany. Then looking around at the people standing next to her, she began to sign. "Starving and mistreating foreigners is no way for Germans to act. Meme, we've got to do something to help them."

That evening, in Jan's apartment, Cato, Meme, and three of their closest friends discussed what they could do. When Cato suggested they smuggle food to the prisoners, the others agreed. Cato and her friend Billie would work out of the Westkreutz station. Meme, Detta Zimmerman, and Tatjane de Bellegarde would operate from the Witzleben stop.

"Every day," Meme recalls, "we got up at 5:00 a.m. and rushed, rushed, rushed, to get to the subway station. Then we waited at the entrance, trying to time our dash down the long flight of stairs to the moment before the last car, which held the prisoners, closed. We'd squeeze inside and inquire in French what they needed. After the initial contact, they'd slip notes into our coat pockets as we hung on to the overhead subway straps. The next morning, we'd stuff their pockets with chunks of bread, cigarettes, sometimes an orange."

At the next stop, the girls hopped off the car, doubled back, and took another subway to school or to work.

Unlike cigarettes, bread was rationed. The girls had to buy it on the black market. At the black market, which shifted from alley to alley, people could buy food and clothing without ration coupons at a very high price. But anyone caught buying or selling there could be sentenced to death. The girls' meager allowances were quickly swallowed up by the exorbitant prices, and Jan and his friends contributed what they could.

Cato was shocked when the Frenchmen told her they had no medicine. To help the prisoners, Hannes stole aspirin and other medicines from the clinic. Whenever he came into the studio, his raincoat pockets bulged with scarce pharmaceuticals.

Like the girls, he was aware that if one of them were caught, they would all be sentenced to death for "aiding the enemy."

One morning, when tiny, blond-haired Detta stepped off the train, a man in black boots and a leather coat, with the death's head insignia on his cap, tapped her on the shoulder. "Can I buy you a drink?"

"I knew better than to say no to an S.S. man," Detta asserts. "I said, 'Yes, thank you,' trying not to show my fear."

As she took his arm, the S.S. man led the eighteen-year-old to a small café and ordered two cognacs.

Detta recounts the rest of the story:

"What you did today was dangerous," the S.S. man told me. "If another S.S. man had seen you, you'd be on your way to a concentration camp. Don't do it again."

I thanked him and, trembling, returned to school.

Later, the girls talked it over, and they all agreed that they couldn't stop. Instead, they switched to different stations. Though they walked around in fear, "that was a part of the times," Miejte says.

As the Nazis began their campaign to round up the Jews of Berlin, Cato became concerned that she was not doing enough.

With her Aunt Emma, Cato became involved in saving a Jewish woman from deportation. When the woman, who was living with a Christian friend, received a notice that she would be picked up the next day, she wrote a suicide note.

The following morning, when the Gestapo came to arrest her, her Christian friend showed them the note and told the Gestapo the woman had jumped into the river. The Gestapo believed her. Many other Jews had committed suicide rather than be deported. The fugitive was really hiding in the attic. To keep her alive, Cato sneaked up the back steps of the apartment house every week, first making sure the janitor was at his party meeting, to deliver the food and vitamins that Emma and Cato's Uncle Hans Schultze-Ritter collected from friends.

As the Gestapo became more and more vigilant in tracking down Jews and opponents of the regime, the number of those in need of rescue ballooned. When a young Jewish student received a notice telling her to prepare for deportation, her fiancé, a medical student, asked Hannes to help spirit her out of Germany.

Hannes gave Cato the task of finding the warm clothing necessary for the girl to be smuggled over the Alps. In wartime, clothing, particularly hiking boots, was in short supply, and it was important to find boots in the girl's size. "Cato had to do it carefully, so as not to arouse suspicions," Meme says. "She had to go from one black market to another until she found the boots, ski jacket, pants, warm sweaters, everything."

Adding to Cato's concerns were the nightly bombings. Meme says, "We got used to going without sleep, because it was constantly interrupted."

Their stepmother, Rali, was also a concern. Rali's father was Jewish, her mother, Christian, and there were rumors that half-Jews would soon be deported to concentration camps. If the Nazis began to round up half-Jews, then Rali would have to be hidden. But where?

Chapter 21

Heinz

When Cato opened the door, she immediately recognized Heinz Strelow. Though she had not seen Heinz since she was a child, she remembered him as the bucktoothed teenager with thick glasses who had bicycled sixty miles from Hamburg to Fischerhude to visit Uncle Fritz. Meme recalls him as "the ugliest man I have ever seen," but Cato was oblivious to his appearance.

A corporal in the army, Strelow was stationed as a prison guard in Berlin. Before the Nazi takeover, Heinz had been a reporter for a Communist newspaper, and Cato was fascinated by his stories of the people he had interviewed.

In 1933, when Hitler came to power, Heinz was arrested for being a member of the Young Communist League and imprisoned in a concentration camp. Just before the war, he was released and drafted into the army. His unit was among the first to invade Poland.

Cato sat on the couch, horrified as Heinz described the Einsatszgruppen, the S.S. killing squads that followed the regular army units. The Einsatszgruppen had orders to wipe out not only

Jews but anyone with a high school education. Priests, teachers, mayors, in some villages, even Boy Scouts were murdered.

Trembling with anger, Cato asked, "How can we allow such things? Isn't there anything we can do?"

Heinz squeezed her hand, "Perhaps."

A few weeks later, he escorted Cato to the home of Dr. John Rittmeister, a psychiatrist. For Cato, the meeting was exhilarating. Like the other young people sprawled on the floor of Rittmeister's living room, she found hope in his message. To overthrow the regime, he said, they had only to urge Germans to read and discuss books on good government and philosophy. Then everyone would join them in working toward restoring a democratic government.

As naive as it seems, Cato and the others wanted to believe it was possible to depose the Nazis without resorting to violence. She also felt a kinship with Rittmeister's wife, Eva, an actress. Like many in the group, Eva was a Communist. But Marie Terwiel and her fiancé, Hans Helmut Himpel, joined because Marie was half-Jewish, and Hitler had forbidden half-Jews and Christians to marry. Though she was a devout Catholic, under Nazi law, Marie could not marry Himpel, a dentist. The other members included Fritz Rehmer, a law student, and his fiancée, Lia Berkowitz.

As the meeting ended, Cato offered to help distribute anti-Nazi posters. Not only did the work have to be done at two or three in the morning, when there were fewer police on the streets, but it had to be done when there was no moon.

Alert to the slightest sound, Cato stood watch. When Heinz finished pasting a sign on the door of the railroad station, he took her hand and drew her towards the stanchion in front of the post office. She marveled over his movements as, cat-like, he led Cato to the next target— Berlin's largest movie house. Instead of the coming attractions, the billboard now flaunted their message, "Germans, you are not alone. Defy the Nazis . . . ."

As dawn began to filter across the sky, Cato and Heinz ducked from doorway to doorway to reach Jan's apartment. Before the posters were discovered and torn down, Cato knew that a few people would see them. Berliners would know that someone, somewhere in their city, stood for decency.

On June 22, 1941, their activities became even more dangerous. German troops attacked the Soviet Union, and Germany declared war on its former ally. Until then, Hitler had hidden his intention to destroy and occupy the Soviet Union. But with the subjugation of Poland and Western Europe, he felt he could wage a war for the entire continent. If he was successful, the Soviet Union's factories, its mines, and its fields rich with wheat and rye would help Hitler and his allies, Japan and Italy, control the world.

Overnight the Nazi propaganda machines reversed themselves and labeled their former Russian allies as "vermin," "rats," and "barbarians." A book issued by the S.S., *Der Untermensch (The Subhuman)*, described the Slavic people (which included most people in the Soviet Union) as the lowest form of animal and not to be trusted. Radio announcers broadcast that the only choice for the German people was "victory or death." Hitler and Göbbels raged that if the Soviets won the war, they would "enslave and starve the German people."

Cato was stunned by this outpouring of hate. She had always admired Russian culture. Tolstoy and Dostoyevsky were two of her favorite authors, and Aunt Emma, who had lived in Russia, had praised its people. How could they suddenly turn into demons?

Not only was Cato terrified by Hitler's attack on Russia, but a few months later, she became even more distraught. Hitler's next plan was to make Berlin *judenrein*, free of Jews.

On the evening of October 12, a Jewish neighbor, who lived in the apartment below, knocked on Jan's door. Both Meme and Cato went to open it. As the woman stood there, trembling, she thrust a heavy package into Cato's hands.

Cato drew her inside, even though it was dangerous to be seen with a Jew.

"I can't stay," the woman said. "I have to get ready. Tomorrow we're being taken away to the

East. The candlesticks belonged to my grandmother. Please keep them until I come back."

Cato promised. But she knew from Heinz and
from soldiers home on leave, who had whispered
about the gassing of Jews, that it was unlikely the
woman would return.

At five the next morning, Cato was awakened
by a noise. She looked out the window. She
saw the woman, her husband, the grandmother,
and the little boy, clinging to his teddy bear,
being led across the courtyard to the police
wagon.

Cato wept as she told Heinz about the deportation. Putting up posters was not enough. They
had to do more.

Chapter 22

Libertas

To Cato, meeting Libertas was like blowing out a birthday candle and having a wish come true. When Libertas came into the ceramic studio to select a vase, Jan introduced her to Cato, "Here's someone I think you would like to meet."

In her green loden suit and feathered fedora, Libertas Schulze-Boysen looked like the poised sophisticate that nineteen-year-old Cato dreamed of becoming. Libertas, the granddaughter of Prince Metternich, worked in the film department of the Ministry of Propaganda. Her job was to decide which foreign films could be exhibited. Since Cato spoke English, Libertas invited her to help preview American films. Cato held her breath, not really believing what she had heard. Then her smile flooded the room.

Meme says, "It was paradise for Cato to see all these foreign films, and Libertas fascinated her. Her husband, Harro Schulze-Boysen, was an official in the Air Ministry. Blond and handsome, Harro, too, came from an aristocratic family."

Despite his high position, Cato knew that if the

Schulze-Boysens were friends of Jan, they were against the Nazis. One evening, in the projection room of the Ministry of Propaganda, Cato wept as she told Libertas the story of the little boy clinging to his teddy bear. Libertas realized that Cato was ripe for recruitment. As the noise of the projector muffled their conversation, Libertas whispered that she and Harro had formed a resistance group. Would Cato and Heinz be willing to join them?

Libertas did not mention that she and Harro were a part of an international spy ring working for the Soviet government. In fact, Harro was the head of the German branch of what the Nazis later dubbed the Red Orchestra.

Harro's position in the Air Ministry was so important that he had access to classified information, including the movements of German troops. This information he funneled to the Russians. He also relayed Hitler's plans to attack Russia on June 22, 1941. Stalin, the Russian dictator, chose to ignore the warning.

Because they were unaware of the Schulze-Boysens' involvement with a foreign power, Cato and Heinz agreed to work with them. To Cato, Libertas and Harro appeared to be fellow idealists, eager to restore democracy.

For the past few months, Cato, Heinz, and Hannes had been a threesome, partying or going to cabarets. When Cato and Heinz asked Hannes to join the group, he declined. "There was something fishy about Harro Schulze-Boysen," he said, and he wanted nothing to do with him.

In an apartment she rented at no. 2 Waitz-strasse, Cato and Heinz began to write and produce flyers to distribute throughout Berlin. The flyers told the truth about the war, information John Rittmeister gathered from monitoring foreign radio channels.

Cato's feeling of joy and excitement mounted as she became involved in every detail, not only in the typing and addressing of the envelopes, but in the wording of the flyers. More and more, she came to admire Heinz's skill as a journalist. Pushed aside were her fears of discovery and imprisonment.

Though Hannes did not want to be involved, he lent Cato and Heinz his typewriter. The Schulze-Boysens provided scarce paper and the gelatin pads Cato used to reproduce the flyers. It was laborious, repetitive work.

Wearing gloves, to prevent leaving fingerprints, Heinz helped her to address the envelopes. Cato had taken the names from telephone books. "To avoid suspicion," Meme says, "she went to several post offices, buying only twenty stamps at each place." Some of the flyers they mailed to offices, some to individuals. Others they left in telephone booths or slipped next to bundles of newspapers at a kiosk on a deserted street corner. It was risky, but Cato felt invulnerable.

The flyers were signed "Agis," after a king of Sparta who had sought to bring democracy to his people. One of the bulletins bore the headline "THE ENTIRE PEOPLE ARE CONCERNED WITH GERMANY'S FUTURE." In the text, the writers accused the Nazis of deceiving the German people by telling them they were winning the war. "Thousands of lives have been lost. . . . Days pass without joy, without a ray of hope . . . The corruption in the administration . . . has reached a nauseating level. . . . All who cherish true values look on . . . how the German name under the . . . swastika is brought to disgrace. . . ."

It urged their fellow Germans "to distribute this letter to the world . . . You are not alone. Give battle with your own hands and then in groups. GERMANY IS OURS TOMORROW."

Though Cato continued to feel exhilarated by her involvement with the resistance, there were moments when she grappled with hopelessness. German tanks led by General Rommel, "the Desert Fox," were sweeping across North Africa in a race to gain control of the Suez Canal and to cut off the British supply route to India and the Far East.

On the Russian front, German tanks, infantry, artillery, and planes bombarded the outskirts of Moscow, intent on capturing the capital of the Soviet Union. Yet despite the seemingly assured victories, the German population was paying a devastating price for these successes. Black-lined death notices, like stacks of coffins, covered more and more pages of the daily newspapers. Most of the obituaries were of young soldiers, "on the Russian front, in the service of the Fatherland."

As Cato's contact with Heinz increased, she realized how much she looked forward to being with him. Despite the seriousness of their work, there was always a book or a joke to share.

Flyer: One of a group of anti-Nazi flyers circulated by Cato Bontjes van Beek.

Though she had vowed to remain faithful to John, Cato found herself thinking less about John and more about Heinz. Finally, she admitted to herself that she no longer was in love with John. It was Heinz with whom she wanted to share her future. But she wasn't sure of his feelings.

One evening, after hours spent in assembling and printing a flyer, they collapsed on the couch. Suddenly she was in Heinz's arms and he was telling her that he loved her. He began to speak about the future–their future. A Germany without Nazis–a place where they could raise children.

To Cato, everything seemed so right, so perfect. She couldn't think of anything more wonderful than being married to Heinz. But to realize their dream–raising children in a free world–they had to continue their activities, no matter how dangerous.

And the risk of being discovered increased as Nazi control of the entire European continent seemed inevitable. By the end of 1941, German victory seemed so assured that Harro Schulze-Boysen told Cato and Heinz to write a flyer asking German workers to sabotage war materials being sent to the front. Cato and Heinz were shocked, and refused. Then Harro ordered them to do it.

Cato stared at Harro in disbelief. He was advocating treason, not passive resistance. The idea of sabotaging German soldiers horrified

Cato. The men at the front were not stick figures. They were Ulrich and the other young men from Fischerhude, and the soldiers on leave with whom she had danced and ice-skated.

Cato felt used and betrayed. "After a fiery confrontation with Harro," Meme says, "Cato and Heinz left the group."

On their own, they vowed to continue their work.

Chapter 23

Just Before Dawn

Hannes was furious when Cato told him she was in love with Heinz. "I wanted to murder him," Hannes says. "I took a knife and waited for him at the corner for three hours, but he never came."

Hannes was not the only one who was disturbed over Cato's preference for Heinz. Olga made a special visit to Berlin hoping to dissuade Cato from becoming involved with him.

"The whole family thought Hannes, who was so cultured, was a much better match for her," Detta says. "Heinz's speech could be crude at times."

Since Cato had always sought her family's approval, she was devastated by Olga's response. At the end of July, Cato made an unannounced visit to Fischerhude. She wanted to persuade her mother that she and Heinz were suited to each other, and she wanted to comfort her mother, since Tim was being drafted into the army.

Unlike the Allied nations, the Nazis did not recognize conscientious objectors, people who, for moral or religious reasons, refused to go to war. In Germany, men either fought or were executed. Tim, though he was morally against war, had no choice.

When Cato left Fischerhude, she promised her mother she would not see Heinz for several weeks. A few days later, she went off for a hiking holiday in the Bavarian Alps. She had to be alone, to sort things out, to determine her true feelings for Heinz. Wandering at her own pace, Cato climbed seven mountains, sleeping at night in the hut on top of each mountain. Walking through a swamp, she slipped off her hiking boots, enjoying the squish of mud between her toes.

The last few days she spent in the tiny village of Lam. From the hut of a peasant woman, she wrote of sharing simple meals of flour soup and dry bread. In a letter she sent to Annita, Cato confessed that "for the first time in three weeks I can write letters again. I feel much better and life looks nice to me. . . . Do you remember our games? . . . We certainly experienced happy times in our fantasy world. I often live again in fantasy. I believe that when one believes strongly, then it becomes real."

Her "vagabond highway days," as Cato called them, ended on August 13. After a brief stop in Fischerhude, she left for Berlin, where she planned to stay with her father. As more and more half-Jews were being rounded up, Rali, whose father was Jewish, had fled to the Harz Mountains.

On September 20, just before dawn, there was a knock on Jan's door. Gestapo! The two men allowed Cato and Jan only enough time to dress.

A neighbor, alerted by the noise, watched from behind the window as the men in long leather coats pushed Jan and Cato into a black Mercedes. Within minutes, the telephone rang at the home of Cato's Aunt Jossi and Uncle Hans Schultze-Ritter. "Cato's gone away," a voice said and hung up. Code words! Cato was under arrest.

Alexanderplatz Prison
September 1942

Hans, Jossi, and Jossi's sister Emma took a taxi to Jan's apartment. The door was sealed with black tape and a sign, "Do Not Enter!"

Olga was in a remote village in the Bavarian Alps, visiting friends. Hans sent a telegram, "Urgent. Come to Berlin."

While they awaited Olga's arrival, Hans went to Gestapo Headquarters. The clerk insisted the S.S. had no information. At the police station, a sergeant waved him away. Emma called the prisons in and around Berlin. Nothing. Cato and Jan had vanished.

Hans contacted friends in the resistance. They reported that others had disappeared within the past few weeks: Harro and Libertas Schulze-Boysen, John Sieg, Arvin Harnack, Adam Kuckholtz. . . . Heinz, too, had been arrested.

In despair, Hans called someone he knew in the Foreign Office. The man advised him to get a lawyer who was a member of the Nazi party.

It was not until a month after her arrest that a prisoner who had just been released came to the Schultze-Ritter apartment, where Olga was staying, with a message from Cato. She and Jan were in Alexanderplatz Prison. "I knew the charges against them were grave," Olga says, "Alexanderplatz was reserved for military offenders, people accused of treason."

She wrote to the superintendent asking for permission to see Cato. In late October, permission was granted.

With her sister Emma, Olga approached the gray stone building. The prison, with its barred windows, stretched across the entire block.

Cato's cheery laugh greeted them as they entered the visiting room "Mama, you're here," Olga remembers her saying.

"I looked at her. Cato's usually ruddy cheeks were pasty-looking from the lack of decent food. And her hands moved constantly, trying to crush the lice crawling through her hair and across the shoulders of her filthy dress, probably the dress she had worn when she was arrested."

Cato assured Olga that at the most, "I'll get five years."

Olga looked around. There were no guards, but she was afraid to speak out. She was sure the room was bugged. "Why else did they leave us alone?" she says. "I thought, the Nazis never give five years. I put my finger to my mouth and told Cato to whisper."

Emma handed Cato the package that had been checked by the guard: clean underwear, apples, and bread.

Cato's bright smile and thank-you filled the room. "Twice a week," she said loudly, so the matron could hear her, "you can pick up my dirty laundry and bring me clean clothing. Take it to the side window." Then she lowered her voice, "Always inspect the seams."

Patting her mother's hand, Cato remained silent over the conditions of her confinement— the constant dampness from moisture dripping off the stone walls, the nightly terror of rats scrambling across the floor and pouncing on her bed, the silence pierced only by bone-chilling screams from some nearby chamber, and the utter, utter darkness when the light disappeared from the narrow window at the top of the cell.

The next day, Olga picked up the laundry. At the Schultze-Ritters', she fingered each seam. From Cato's pajamas, Olga extracted the tissue-thin paper that Cato had, despite her handcuffs, rolled into a narrow sliver. In the letter, Cato tried to reassure her family: "The main thing is that you don't have too much worry about me. I turn my thoughts off completely so I will not find the cell too oppressive."

In the same note, Cato stressed that her chief concern was "that Papa will be set free. I find it frightful that he is here in prison, too." Later, she wrote:

November 1942

How does it go with me? Ach,
Mama, I think actually not about why

> I am here but about you. About the
> sense of family, what it means. . . .
> How poor a person is who stands
> alone in the world. I am thankful I
> have all of you.

Cato added to the letter "a few requests: vita-
min pills, a blouse with long sleeves, cream or
skin oil, slippers, because I suffer from cold feet."
As she did in other letters from prison, she
signed it with her nickname, Dodo.

In December, when Olga was again permitted
to see Cato, Jan and a prison official were in the
room. The man began to question Olga about
Jan's involvement with the resistance.

"When they asked me about Jan, I said, 'He is
the most unpolitical man I know. All he cares
about are his ceramic pots,'" Olga relates. "The
authorities were amazed that a divorced woman
did not denounce her former husband."

Cato, too, testified that Jan was not interested
in politics. She swore that he knew nothing of
her activities.

Just before Christmas, Jan was released.

Cato remained. Handcuffed and in solitary
confinement, Cato was frightened. No formal
charges had been filed against her. What would
be her fate?

CHAPTER 25

A Friend in the S.S.

Without light, without paper, without a book, there was nothing to do except think and sing. For weeks before Christmas, she and Meme had always sung Christmas carols as they walked back and forth to school or to work. Now, to keep up her morale and to inspire hope in the other prisoners, Cato sang, her voice soaring through the barred window and down into the courtyard, "Silent night, holy night, all is calm, all is bright. . . ." The prisoners, crowded together shoulder to shoulder, looked up to see the origin of this miracle.

As she sang, Cato was transported back to Christmases in Fischerhude. Their coats buttoned against the falling snow and their scarves wound around their necks and covering their ears, she, Meme, and Tim leading the caroling as the family trudged through the drifts to Haina and Fritz's house.

In the glow of the fireplace, they opened presents, usually a book for Cato. Then, with Haina on the violin and Olga at the piano, the music of Mozart filled the room as they munched *lebkuchen* and raised their glasses to the holiday season.

Now, every morning and every evening, Cato stood before the barred window, her voice reminding the prisoners that there was such a thing as Christmas. The guards were so impressed with Cato's courage that they did not attempt to stop her.

As she sang, Cato searched for Heinz in the tightly crowded courtyard. But she never found him. One man, though, waved to her. She waved back. He waved again. Then she wrote her name with her finger. "You?" she signed. He signaled back, "Helmut Nievert."

That evening, after all the prisoners had been served their usual meal of a lump of bread and a bowl of watery cabbage soup, the guard returned to Cato's cell. With his finger on his mouth, he led her through the dark corridor to another part of the prison. As the guard unlocked the door, Helmut Nievert extended his hand in welcome.

Helmut Nievert was not the usual prisoner. An S.S. officer, he had been sentenced to jail for stealing gasoline to take a young woman on a ride through the countryside. Cato's courage intrigued him, and he asked the guard to arrange a meeting.

Soon they were chatting about her favorite author, Dostoyevsky, and about his favorite painters, van Gogh and Rembrandt. Helmut's father was an architect who had been a member of the Social Democratic party before the Nazis' takeover. As a member of the Hitler Youth,

Nievert had scoffed at his father's ideas. Mesmerized by Hitler, he later joined the S.S.

As one secret visit followed another, Nievert became concerned over the swollen purple spots covering Cato's fingers and ears. He knew they were a sign of chillblains. In a letter to Frau Weber, the wife of a friend, he asked her to "call telephone number 312729 and tell Frau Bontjes-Breling that her daughter Cato lies in an unheated cell and urgently needs warm things."

At the same time, Cato noticed that Helmut shivered as he talked. The Gestapo did not believe in wasting money on blankets or heat for prisoners. The dampness dripping from the walls intensified the cold. Helmut shrugged off Cato's concern, saying he missed cigarettes more than anything else.

In her next letter to Olga, Cato requested that her mother bring Nievert a blanket and cigarettes. When Olga brought the package to Nievert, the S.S. officer was touched by her kindness in the midst of her own troubles.

Even though charges had not been brought against her, and her future was uncertain, Cato looked forward to her nightly meetings with Nievert. One evening, she was amazed to hear him say that Hitler had duped the German people. After the war, Helmut declared, he would work with her to help make Germany democratic.

Cato was overjoyed. If Helmut, an S.S. man, felt that the Nazis were bad for Germany, perhaps Ulrich would one day realize that Hitler was destroying their country.

As December passed without any charges being brought against her, Cato grew more hopeful. After all, she had not been a member of the Rote Kapelle, the Red Orchestra, and she had not worked for a foreign government. It was a shock when her lawyer appeared and announced that her trial would take place on January fourteenth.

The lawyer, a member of the Nazi party, assured Cato that at the most, she would be sentenced to three to five years in prison. Under German law there were two charges related to treason. The most serious one, *landesverrat*, involved an attempt to overthrow the government on behalf of a foreign power. If convicted, the accused was condemned to death.

However, the lesser charge of *hochverrat* of which Cato was accused, did not carry a death penalty. According to the law, *hochverrat* was defined as an attempt to overthrow the government for reasons of personal belief, such as not agreeing with the way the leaders ran the country. Several times her lawyer reassured her that the crime of *hochverrat* carried no more than three to five years. Even if she were found guilty, she would be alive at the end of the war! In her naïveté, Cato never doubted him.

The Butcher of Berlin

A s incredible as it seems, Cato walked into the courtroom smiling. Not only was she seeing Heinz for the first time in months, but her lawyer had assured her that any sentence would be a light one. Heinz rushed over to embrace her. The guards separated them.

The faces of the other defendants—Liane Berkowitz, Fritz Rehmer, Hannelore and Fritz Thiel, Professor Werner Krauss, Ursula Goetze, Otto Gollnow, and Heinz—were grim.

From the beginning, the trial was a farce. Like a tiger, Dr. Manfred Roeder, the prosecuting attorney, stalked back and forth across the courtroom, roaring and shaking his finger at defendants and judges. "The Butcher of Berlin," as Roeder was called for always seeking the death penalty, drowned out the defendants as they tried to speak in their own behalf. Shaking his fists, Roeder outshouted their lawyers whenever they attempted to raise a point. His robes billowing, the prosecutor paced back and forth across the courtroom, his indignation intimidating the judges.

When one, a general, dared to suggest there

was insufficient evidence to support a charge of treason against Cato, Roeder's rage silenced him.

At the end of the first day, Cato realized that the charges were much more serious than she had thought. Neither she nor the other defendants were aware that a retroactive law had been passed by Hitler. The crime of *hochverrat,* for which they were being tried, now carried the death penalty. Those who had "lifted even a finger" against the Nazi regime were to be condemned to death.

Heinz, too, sensed that with Roeder as the prosecuting attorney, he had little chance of surviving. His one hope was that Cato would be spared. After the second day of trial, a guard slipped a note from Heinz to Cato:

January 15, 1943

In spite of the harm they have brought us, the past two days were comforting, since I was once again near you. . . .

And Dodo . . . if I do not carry as much blame for your fate as the senate president reproached me with, I am not free of responsibility and blame for you. I hope you will forgive me. . . .

When you are once again free, then live this beautiful life at double strength. . . . You have the purest and best and most innocent heart. . . .

Heinz

Cato, with her incredible optimism, refused to accept the fact that either she or Heinz was doomed. Surely, she wrote to Meme, the judges would realize that what they had done had been dictated by their consciences. They were never a part of the Red Orchestra.

After two and a half days of trial, the defendants were told to rise for sentencing. As Heinz grasped her hand, Cato heard the verdict.

Cato Bontjes van Beek: death!

Heinz Strelow: death!

Liane Berkowitz: death!

Fritz Rehmer: death!

Fritz Thiel: death!

Werner Krauss: death!

Ursula Goetze: death!

Only Otto Gollnow and Hannelore Thiel, because of their youth, received prison terms.

The defendants stood there, stunned.

Heinz put his arms around Cato. The guards rushed up, pulled them apart, and placed a white band around their upper arms. The black letters, TD, revealed their sentences. *TD, todeskandidat*, candidate for death!

Cato's face, as gray as her sack-shaped dress, mirrored her fear and disbelief. In a trance, she followed the guard back to her cell.

As Cato sank down on her cot, she began to tremble, overwhelmed by rage, fear, hopelessness, denial. Surely her life would not end at twenty-two!

Her only hope was for Olga to make an appeal. But how would she know of her sentence? No one from the family was notified of the trial. Even her lawyer was forbidden to report that it had taken place.

Somehow, Cato found the strength to write an appeal to Hitler. In a letter that she later sent to her mother, Cato revealed a portion of her plea:

February 1943,

I told him that the wonderful thing for me is to be able to help others. That was my final word in court. . . . In spite of this, I believe to the end that a miracle will give me back my life. . . .

Cato, fearful that the sentence might be carried out immediately, added:

. . . I cannot yet comprehend that this will be a farewell letter. . . . In me there is only love for you and for all other people. I am completely free of anger or hate. . . . I know that man is good, and that makes dying easier. . . .

Until then, Cato had always felt in control of her life. Now she was powerless. She could only pray that Olga would be successful.

She opened her Bible and turned to the Gospels. Slowly, she read from Matthew, "Holy are those with clean hearts and these will God bless."

CHAPTER 27

A Glimmer of Hope

For six weeks, Cato sat in prison, not knowing whether Olga knew she had been sentenced to death. Since prisoners were not allowed to receive or send mail, Cato could only continue to smuggle letters to Olga in her laundry. And hope. Despite her sentence, Cato refused to believe she would be executed. In a letter to her mother dated March 2, 1943, she wrote, "If they had taken me the first few days, I would have gone willingly, but now a great will to live has swelled within me... We follow the events in the world with great anxiety ... with such hope ... perhaps we will all have luck."

In the same note, Cato added that Heinz's case was the first one to be brought before the court, "and then mine":

March 2, 1943

It was so nerve-racking and demanding.... Heinz and I ... built a case for ourselves stating that we had nothing to do with the other cases....

You can imagine my surprise when the prosecutor demanded the death penalty.... I did not have the

> impression that the four generals and
> the senate president wanted to pass
> this sentence. . . . It . . . was ordered
> from above. Anyone who had lifted a
> small finger for Harro Schulze-Boysen
> had to pay with his life. That Heinz
> and I had broken off and had parted
> with disagreement [from the Schulze-
> Boysens] . . . played no role.

In an effort to save her own life, Libertas Schulze-Boysen had blurted out the names of everyone she knew. She hoped that by sacrificing friends and acquaintances, she would remain alive. On December 22, 1942, shortly after her trial, Libertas was beheaded.

Libertas's betrayal doomed many others. Through the guard, Cato learned that thirty-seven people had been sentenced to death. Others awaited trial.

The reason for the death sentence soon became clear. The German armies that had swept so triumphantly across Russia during the summer had been stopped at Stalingrad. In November, the Russian army had launched a fierce counterattack and encircled the German forces. In February 1943, in danger of annihilation, the Germans surrendered.

Hitler was enraged by this defeat. He demanded that anyone who had helped the enemy in any way be executed. Cato, unaware of the order, continued to hope for a commutation of her sentence. In March, she wrote to her mother:

> My thoughts are absolutely in the future. . . .
>
> Actually I have always had luck in life. Why shouldn't I have it this time? ... You must start the clemency plea very carefully. I am not permitted to tell you anything and the lawyers can't either. . . . I am still alive and it certainly won't come about. . . .

In the same letter, she enclosed the phone number of the sister and brother of Marie Terwiel, a young woman who had also been convicted of being a member of the Red Orchestra. Cato asked Olga to meet them and tell them that Marie, too, had been condemned to death. Adding a postscript, Cato reminded Olga not to reveal anything on the telephone, only to arrange a meeting place. "You don't know whether the mail or telephones are tapped," Cato warned.

Though the news of Cato's sentence shocked and terrified her, Olga refused to give up hope. She approached everyone she knew who might have some influence with Hitler and asked the person to write an appeal for clemency. Anna Sokol, a woman who had nursed Hitler back to health after he was wounded in World War I, was among those who did.

Even before she had been sentenced, Cato's flying group had written in her behalf to prison officials:

November 26, 1942

We have learned that our flying comrade, Cato Bontjes van Beek is awaiting sentence. . . .

We have known her since 1937 . . . [and] we have noticed that she embraced the idea of flying with such intensity that it gives us the impression that she could also enter into other areas with such drive that she could lose her perspective. . . . We cannot believe . . . that her sense of justice and reason would permit her to do anything worthy of sentencing.

We ask the court to consider that Cato has made mistakes in youthful zeal . . . and that it should not exclude from her the possibility of reform.

Olga added a copy of the letter to the petitions she obtained from the Council of Churches, Lolo, and many friends in the art world.

After months of not being allowed to have visitors, Cato was elated when Olga received permission to see her. Olga shudders as she recalls the waiting room with its gray walls and barred windows. "I watched as Cato, accompanied by a guard, entered from a side door. Though her skin was sallow and mottled from an improper diet, she seemed in good spirits. She blew a kiss as she walked across the room."

The guard seated Cato behind a long wooden table. Olga sat on the other side, forbidden to stretch across the barrier to embrace her daughter. Their eyes met.

"You can say anything you want," the guard whispered to Olga. "But if you say something you shouldn't, I'll warn you to stop."

"In the fifteen minutes I was permitted to see her," Olga says, "I assured her that we were doing everything possible to appeal the verdict. And I told her I was leaving the next day for Fischerhude to see Gauleiter Peper."

Olga felt that Peper, the Nazi official in charge of her local district, would have some influence with Hitler.

Despite their political differences, Olga and the gauleiter had remained friends. Cato was sure he would help her. Filled with hope, she returned to her cell.

Chapter 28

The Appeal

Gauleiter Heinrich Peper was Cato's last hope. Even though he was a Nazi, the local official admired Olga and, in the past, had dropped by to discuss art. Surely, he would use his influence to help commute Cato's sentence. He had known her since she was a little girl.

With bitterness, Olga recalls her visit to Peper's office. When she asked him to appeal to Hitler to reduce Cato's sentence to life in prison, he replied, "No, it wouldn't be fair to Cato. She'd spend the rest of her life in jail."

"I couldn't say, 'everyone knows Germany is losing the war, in a few years, she'll be free,'" Olga recalls.

Heartbroken, yet unwilling to stop her efforts to save Cato, Olga returned to Berlin. She had obtained additional petitions from prominent people in Bremen and Hamburg. Surely, Hitler could be swayed.

The next morning, she took the petitions to the office of the prosecuting attorney, Manfred Roeder. Despite his reputation as the Butcher of Berlin, perhaps he might, just this once, be lenient.

A clerk led Olga down the marble corridors to Roeder's office. Without offering her a seat, the secretary told her to wait.

"As I stood there," she recalls, "I heard the sharp staccato of footsteps striding down the hall. Then a peal of devilish laughter."

A man entered the room. "I recognized Roeder from newspaper photographs—sharp nose, like a terrier, and dark hair."

He didn't see Olga at first. When he finally noticed her, he didn't say, "Hello," just a gruff "What do you want?"

"I looked at him," Olga says. "I wanted to say something, but I thought, with such a man, any word is in vain. Anyone who can laugh like that and who looks so cruel, any word would be in vain. I just said, 'Here is a plea for clemency.'

"'Put it down,' he said, not looking at me.

"I put it down. Another man said, 'You can leave now.' I slammed the door."

As Olga walked toward the exit, someone came up to her. He whispered that Admiral Bastian was going to present the appeals to Hitler the next day. "I thought, at least one person with compassion."

An overwrought Olga returned to the Schultze-Ritters. Her sister Jossi had picked up the laundry from the prison, and from inside the seams of Cato's slip, Jossi extracted a letter:

March 1943

. . .I heard that the proceedings will be reopened, that the sentences were too high. Consider the post-trial examination before another president as being favorable. . . . I am not really badly off: just that homesickness and my longing for you grabs me.

Isn't it nonsense, I here, and Tim a soldier in Russia? It's a crazy feeling when the air raid alarm sounds and we are locked up in our cells. . . . Have no fear. I will certainly live. . . .

You could enclose a flower each Monday. I have such a longing for them. . . .

In the same letter, Cato wrote of "a great hunger . . . the slices of bread get thinner and thinner." The prisoners were not the only ones to suffer because of food being diverted to the armed forces. Civilian rations, too, were cut. It was almost impossible to find milk, eggs, meat, fruit, and vegetables in the shops. Only on the black market were those foods available, and few people had the money to pay the outrageous prices.

Cato also asked Olga to try to smuggle a Polish grammar inside her laundry, "to provide some activity"; a pencil, as hers was down to the stub; and copies of the newspaper the *Reich on Satur-*

day, "for we follow everything with extreme interest and everything passes much too slowly. . . . Mama, if only everything would be over. But I will be brave. Your great love gives me the strength for it."

A few weeks later, Cato heard the terrifying news that Hitler had rejected all appeals for leniency. German troops were being driven back on the Russian front, and Hitler blamed every German for his failure to conquer the Soviet Union. If Germany were to go down in defeat, Hitler saw no reason to save the lives of those who opposed him.

Still, Cato refused to give up hope or to stop singing. The war *could* be over before the sentence was carried out. With Marie Terwiel, she began to discuss the Bible. Marie was a devout Catholic and believed that prayer could bring about miracles.

Cato desperately wanted to believe in miracles. She turned to the Gospels.

Chapter 29

Escape?

The sharp knock jolted Olga out of the deep sleep into which she had finally fallen. For weeks, she had tossed in her bed, her mind constantly seeking more and more people to contact in Cato's behalf. Exhausted, she felt as though she had come to a dead end.

Olga groped for a flashlight. Who could it be? She began to tremble. Had Cato's sentence been carried out? She threw on her robe and opened the door.

In the dim light, she saw the black boots and the uniform of the S.S. Dear God!

Helmut Nievert put his finger to his lips and stepped inside. Jossi, Hans, and Emma, half dazed, staggered into the living room, the buttons on Hans's bathrobe askew.

They stared at Helmut in disbelief, unaware that he had served his sentence and had just been released from prison. Assuring them that Cato was still alive, he told them he had a plan to rescue her, but he needed Olga's help.

In two days, Cato had a dental appointment to treat an abscessed tooth. The dentist's office was the only one in the prison with two exits. One led to the corridor inside the prison; the other opened to the street.

Helmut's plan was to enter the dentist's office with an S.S. uniform in Cato's size. Cato would go into the closet, put it on, and then disappear into an S.S. limousine that would be waiting outside the door. Five other S.S. men would accompany them. They would drive Cato across the border and hide her until after the war.

For the first time in months, Olga was filled with hope. "But it's dangerous," she cautioned. "For you, for the others."

Nievert assured her that all the details had been worked out. The other S.S. men were fed up with Hitler, and they felt Cato's sentence was unjust.

There was only one problem, Helmut said, mindful of her feelings about Heinz. Cato might not agree to be rescued. Olga must write to her and persuade Cato to let Helmut make the attempt. Her sentence could be carried out at any moment, and the note had to be written that morning and brought to the wife of one of Helmut's friends. Her husband would deliver the letter to a prison guard who would smuggle it to Cato.

Helmut left, promising to come back the next evening.

Within the hour, Olga delivered the note.

In prison, Cato stood beside the window reading and rereading the message the guard had slipped under the door. At first, her spirits soared. Then, thinking of Heinz and the others, she questioned whether she alone had the right to survive. Once again, she took out the letter Heinz had smuggled to her during the trial:

> . . . It would be easier for me if I could know that you, Dodo, remain alive. . . . If it be so . . . when you are once again free, then live this beautiful life at double strength and . . . don't be sad about me. . . .

Could she do it? Or would she always be haunted by the knowledge that she alone had lived?

Early the next morning, Olga went to the home of Helmut's friend. The woman handed her Cato's letter. Olga hurried down the stairs and ducked into the doorway of a shop. Tearing open the envelope, her eyes blurred as she read Cato's response. It contained only one sentence: "What about the others?"

That evening, when Helmut returned to the apartment, Olga showed him the note.

"Only Cato," Olga remembers him saying. "With the nightly bombings, the troops retreating from the Russian front, the S.S. won't bother to look for one person. If all of them escape, every one will be hunted down."

Olga no longer has the note, only the memory of Cato's reply: "I cannot abandon the others."

Chapter 30

Easter, 1943

Cato was frightened. The morning of March 30, the guard informed her she was being transferred to another prison. Was this the end? She trembled as she gathered her things. With several other young women who had been tried as members of the Red Orchestra, Cato climbed into the police wagon. No one spoke as the black van traveled through the bombed-out streets of Berlin. After a few blocks, the wagon stopped. The girls got out and followed the guard into the women's prison on Kantstrasse (Kant Street).

Despite the gloomy, restricted atmosphere of Alexanderplatz Prison, it had been familiar to her. She knew the guards and they respected her. Now she was entering a strange, unknown place. Was this really the end? No, she tried to reassure herself. Executions usually took place at Ploetzensee Prison. Did it mean her sentence would be commuted, that she would live? With hope, disbelief, and fear she asked the guards what was happening. They knew nothing.

But in her next letter, Cato wrote that she found the new prison more pleasant than the previous one. Here, she was allowed to go into the exercise yard for half an hour each day. In the five months in Alexanderplatz, her only view of the sky had been from her barred window. Now, during the short period she was outdoors, she could gaze directly at the clouds.

To Cato, the crowded square was a source not only of fresh air but of information on the world outside the prison. As the inmates circled, shoulder to shoulder, around and around the tiny yard, she heard that American troops had landed in North Africa and that German troops in Russia were continuing to retreat. When the prisoners heard the news, they were jubilant. Surely the war would end before their sentences could be carried out.

In the Kantstrasse Prison, Cato was no longer alone during the day. Every morning, another prisoner came into her cell to help assemble pilot lights for use in gas stoves. Though this was slave labor, Cato didn't mind. She relished being able to talk to another human being. They spent hours discussing the books they were permitted to borrow from the prison library. Here, inmates were allowed to read at the end of the workday and on Sundays. To Olga, she mentioned a book by the French philosopher Pascal and added, "I know that the love of mankind will not die in me. I will have to the last the conviction that man is still good. That . . . reconciles . . . and comforts me."

Despite her fear of execution, Cato, like a child at a summer camp, always ended her letters with "send me's." This time, her request was for dark blue darning wool, a red blouse, and if possible, a brush. "I need a daily body brushing for my blood circulation," Cato added.

As long as Cato included the "send me's," Olga thought, Cato believed she would live.

When Easter came, and she was still alive, Cato took it as a good sign. Easter had always been a special time in Fischerhude. To Ulrich, who had written to her from the Netherlands and told her of his concern for her, Cato sent an immediate reply.

April 26, 1943

> You were a great comfort to me . . .
> that all of you believed in me and had
> not forsaken me. . . .

> Now, at Easter time, I think of . . .
> the many Easter eggs we painted each
> year and then laid either by the
> Schmidts in the nests at the foot of
> the great oak tree or in the garden
> under the raspberry bushes by the
> arbor. . . . I believe with the firmness
> of stone that these times will come
> again.

Your Dodo

To Cato, Easter, too, was synonomous with music. She was particularly fond of Bach's "Passion of St. Matthew," which dramatizes the story of Easter. "A few days ago," Cato wrote to

Olga, "I dreamed I heard it. . . . It is quite wonderful that a mortal man was able to create it. When one hears such things, one knows there is no death."

More and more, Cato was finding strength in the Bible. The same day that Cato wrote to Ulrich, she sent a letter to Tim:

April 26, 1943

> I asked Mama to listen to "The Passion of St. Matthew" for the three of us . . . also to "The Art of the Fugue." I often sing or whistle themes from this piece. . . . It is remarkable how this heavenly music binds us. . . . I read the New Testament again and again with completely new eyes. . . . When one has the Bible by his side . . . one needs no other book. . . . My faith, which has slumbered in me until now, I have truly discovered.

Dodo

On May 6, Cato's faith was tested. Heinz and several others were taken to Ploetzensee Prison and beheaded. As Cato sat in her cell, mourning, she realized that she must prepare herself to accept the same fate.

"Still, she continued to sing and to speak to the other prisoners, tapping on the walls, trying to give them courage," Meme says. "As she moved toward death, the guards said she became almost other wordly.

Olga collapsed when she heard that several more members of the Red Orchestra had been executed. The Gestapo had forbidden the release of their names. Was Cato among them? Hans contacted friends in the resistance for information. Cato was still alive.

Within the next week, Olga's hopes of Cato surviving the war increased. On May 13, German troops in North Africa surrendered, and Germany was retreating on the Russian front. Any sensible ruler would have realized it was time to ask for peace, to prevent his forces from being completely wiped out.

But Hitler regarded each defeat on the battlefield as a personal betrayal. In his rage, he refused to consider any appeals for clemency. He kept repeating, "Anyone who has lifted a finger against Germany must die."

Still, Olga prayed that Cato would be spared. Hans had a friend in a high position who was trying to obtain Cato's release. If the Allied forces moved swiftly enough, the war could be over in a few months.

In June, Olga panicked when she learned that Cato had been transferred to a third prison. Was this the end? For months she had been unable to see her daughter. As a last resort, Olga sent a telegram to Tim on the Russian front. Surely the prison warden would not deny a soldier on leave a visit with his sister?

CHAPTER 31

The Visit

Olga was taking a chance, contacting Tim. He was an advance scout in the German army, which was battling for control of the Donets Basin in Russia and was in the thick of the fighting.

When the telegram arrived, a compassionate commander granted Tim a month's leave. As soon as she received word Tim was coming, Olga wrote to the head of the prison. Because Tim was a soldier, the warden granted them special permission to see Cato for fifteen minutes.

In his uniform, eighteen-year-old Tim escorted Olga and Meme inside the prison.

Meme shudders as she speaks of the visit: "It was such a big, frightful room, cold and dark. We waited. Then Cato was brought in. She was wearing pants and a gray dress. When she saw us, she showed great joy and beamed. I couldn't reach over to embrace her. There was a table between us. Cato stood on one side with the guard. We stood on the other."

For Tim, the visit was a nightmare: "I saw the brown armband with *TD*, death candidate, on it. Coming from the battlefield, it was hard for me, after all the dead bodies I had seen. Her face was gray from the bad food, and she was crying terribly. For me, for her, we couldn't talk about anything."

Then the matron tapped Cato on the arm.

To Meme, Cato seemed to suddenly disappear. "Then, just as suddenly, Cato came back and waved at us with a look I will never forget. Before she disappeared, I asked Cato, 'How long will you be here?' And she said, 'Till then,' and pointed to the brown band on her arm."

That night, Cato wrote to Olga to apologize for crying:

> June 20, 1943

> . . . I reproach myself bitterly for making it so difficult for you and Tim by my crying. . . . Perhaps it was the unfortunate circumstances that day, since the tears came to me in the morning during the exercise period when I saw the blue sky and white clouds.

> My dear Mama, you must give no more thought to my crying, since my joy always triumphs knowing you are so near. . . .

How often in the past months have
I longed for the moment I would see
Tim . . . . And now I hope and pray
this was not the last time. . . .

Dodo

On August 5, 1943, a guard came to Cato's cell
and told her she was being transferred to another
prison.

Chapter 32

Requiem

On August 5, 1943, Cato Bontjes van Beek entered the executioner's chamber. Her nightmare of March 1939 had come true. She was the last of the thirteen young women in the transport to Ploetzensee Prison to be beheaded.

S.S. policy forbade anyone from revealing the deaths of those convicted of treason. Their bodies were simply "disposed of."

August Ohm, the prison chaplain, was so moved by Cato's courage that he defied the S.S. order. Immediately after the execution, he called Hans Schultze-Ritter to tell him of Cato's death. An air raid prevented Hans, Jossi, and Emma from leaving for Fischerhude until the next morning.

They arrived in Fischerhude just as the postman was delivering a letter from Pastor Ohm. It was August 6, Olga's birthday. Olga opened the envelope. Inside were the pastor's report of Cato's final hours and three letters: one to Olga, one to Mietje, and one to Tim.

With trembling hands, Olga silently read the pastor's letter:

Report of Dr. August Ohm,
Institution Chaplain, prison,
Moabit, Berlin—August 5, 1943

Cato was taken from her free hour. . . .

Cato did not deceive herself. . . . The transport car had taken four trips on this day. Cato was on the last trip.

Chaplain Ohm awaited them all at the last stop. . . . Cato went calmly, upright, and with raised eyes through the large gate that closed behind her. . . . There she was informed for the first time that all pleas for clemency had been refused. . . .

She said her farewells to the thirteen young persons, who were all in one room. . . .

Then she asked to write three letters: to Meme, Tim, and Mama.

Chaplain Ohm left the room so as not to disturb her. . . .

When she finished her writing, she put down the pen and said, . . . "Now I would like to take communion." Chaplain Ohm gave her communion . . . and she recited the Lord's Prayer with him. . . .

 . . . From her window, she could see a small bit of sky that this day was very clear and blue. Glancing at the sky, she remarked, "It seems so incredible. . . ."

Then she said, "I have no hate and bear no one any ill will. I love mankind. . . .

". . . If only hate were wiped out and people came to God! We would not need to creep out of the world like thieves."

Then she took Chaplain Ohm's hands and held them firmly, smiled, and said, "Hold my mother's hands so firmly for me when you see her!"

Marianne ran to the Schmidts' house. As Haina, Maria, and little Olga entered the house, they joined Amelie, Meme, Marianne, Hans, Jossi, and Emma to form a circle of love, with Olga at its center. Her eyes too full to read, Olga handed Cato's letter to Hans. Softly, he read it aloud:

August 5, 1943

My dear, dear Mama,

I had believed that I could write this letter to you as a birthday letter but it will be my last to you. . . . I will be among the living for only a few more hours . . . .

But I am very composed and have completely reconciled myself to my fate. . . . It gives me great strength to be with you in my thoughts, with Tim in Russia, and with Meme, and with all the other loved ones.

. . . My heart is so full of thanks to you and of the love that I leave to all of you. . . . My beloved Mama, I hope so much that you will overcome this pain that is caused by my death, and through it become greater yet in your art. . . .

It is a shame that I leave nothing in this world except for a memory of me. . . . I know that I have you to thank for my strength and I am so thankful to you. . . .

Recently in church I heard a little Bach piece on the organ—you know what that meant to me. . . .

. . . I really have no need to write so much. For I sense now so vividly that you always know all that is unsaid. . . .

I am always with you, my dearest Mama.

Your Dodo

Cato Bontjes van Beek, age twenty-two.

It was some time before Meme could bring herself to open her letter. "I knew that if I had still been in Berlin when Cato was arrested, I would have been arrested, too," she says. "They usually took the whole family. Now, Cato was dead, and I was alive."

August 5, 1943

My beloved Meme,

. . . You must leave aside in life
everything that does not carry you
forward spiritually. There is so much
that is useless; unfortunately one
learns this too late. . . .

Death is not really a separation, and
what is time? Someday we shall all
be together again.

In my thoughts I embrace you and
am always with you,

With deepest love,

Your sister, Dodo.

Tim's letter awaited his return from the Russian
front. In August 1943, he was wounded in the
hand. A few months later, he reached
Fischerhude.

August 5, 1943

My dearest, my good Tim,

I really don't have to keep telling
you how dear you are to me and how
my thoughts are with you. It was so
wonderful to be able to see you once
more. How tall you have grown and
how strong!

. . . Continue to live in your music: I
know perfectly well that someday you
will accomplish a great deal. A while

ago, I sang the theme of the fifth
Brandenburg concerto to myself, and
I still remember all your Bach pieces.

My good Tim, I am not at all sad
and love you all so very much, and
may God always protect you.

Much, much love,

Your sister, Dodo

It was the custom in the village to ring the
church bells when someone died. Over the past
year, the bells had tolled to announce the death
of a farmer's son on the battlefield or of a villager
killed in an air raid. Cato's friend Pastor Tidow
was serving in the army. A district supervisor of
churches now administered several parishes in
the area. To the supervisor, Cato also had been a
fighter. When Amelie brought him the news, he
rang the bells.

Some villagers considered Cato a traitor. They
reported the supervisor to the Gestapo. He was
arrested and put in prison. A friend of the family, Johanna Eichler, protested the superintendent's arrest, and she was jailed. Eventually both
were released.

A short time later, news reached Fischerhude of
Ulrich's death on the Russian front. Once more
the bells tolled across the fields and rivers of
Fischerhude.

Today, the little lane that surrounds the church
has been named the Cato Bontjes van Beek Weg

(Way). Inside the church, beneath a stained glass window, rests a book of remembrance. It lists the names of those from the village who gave their lives for their country. Cato's name is among them.

On August 5, 1993, two events marked the fiftieth anniversary of Cato's death. In Achim, Germany, a high school was renamed the Cato Bontjes van Beek Schule so that young people of today might be inspired by her courage.

On the same date, in Bremen, a square was dedicated in her name. Helmut Schmidt, her childhood friend and the former chancellor of Germany, delivered the address, praising her heroism and her sacrifice for her country.

APPENDIX

CHRONOLOGY

World Events

Nov 1918

WW l ends. Weimar Republic replaces monarchy.

1920s

Conflict between Communist and fascist groups in Germany.
Inflation in 1923-1924 wipes out savings and causes great hardship.

1930

World wide depression.
Vast unemployment in Germany.
Struggle between political parties.

1933

Nazis seize control of Germany. Concentration camps established.
Enabling Act deprives Germans of civil rights.

1934

Hitler Youth Organizations formed.
Replaces all existing Youth organizations. All youth pressured to join.
National Labor Service Act requires young people to give six months service on farms or in industries.

Cato Bontjes van Beek

November 14, 1920, Cato Bontjes van Beek born in Fischerhude, Germany, into family of Social Democrats.

Family friend, Theodor Lessing, murdered by Nazis. Other friends sent to concentration camps.

Cato refuses to join Hitler Youth.
Her cousin Ulrich, joins Nazi Storm Troopers, the Brownshirts.

1935

Military conscription reintroduced.

Cato attends secretarial school.

1936

Olympics in Berlin.

Cato outraged by Hitler's snub of black athletes.

1937

Germany and Italy sign military assistance pact.
German air force fights in Spain.

Cato visits England.

1938

Germany annexes Austria.
Munich pact forces Czechoslovakia to give Sudetenland to Germany.

Cato returns, questioned by Gestapo.

Crystal Night. Nationwide program against Jews.

Cato's family helps to hide Jews.

1939

Germany seizes rest of Czechoslovakia.
Russia and Germany sign non-aggression pact. Preparations for war increase.

Cato has prophetic dream of being executed.

Hitler demands Danzig and Polish Corridor from Poland. He is refused.

Cato moves to Berlin to work for father to avoid work in munitions plant.

Germany invades and conquers Poland.
France and England declare war on Germany.

1940

Holland, Norway, Denmark invaded.

Cato begins compulsory labor service.

Germany launches attack in West. Battle Of Dunkirk.
France surrenders.

After return to Berlin, helps French prisoners of war.

Battle of Britain begins.
Massive air attacks against England.

Helps Jews to escape from Germany.

1941

Operation Barbarossa.
Germany invades Russia.
German Jews ordered to wear
Yellow Star.
Deportation of Jews increase.
Germany declares war on
U.S.A.

Cato helps Jews with food
and clothing.
Becomes involved in anti-
Nazi resistance group. Prints
and distributes leaflets.

1942

Allies bomb Berlin day and
night.
Wannsee Conference sets the
"Final Solution:" the annihilation of Jews".
German forces in Russia
stopped at Stalingrad.

Cato's brother drafted, sent to
Russia.
Cato's stepmother who is
half-Jewish goes into hiding.
In September, Cato is arrest-
ed, charged with treason.

1943

German army surrenders at
Stalingrad.
Begins withdrawal from
Russia.
Hitler demands death penalty
for all convicted of treason.

Cato and boyfriend convicted
of treason.
Cato's mother seeks clemency
for Cato.
Cato's cousin killed on
Russian front.
Cato executed, August 5,
1943.

Glossary

Allies: A World War II military alliance organized by Great Britain, France, Canada, Australia, New Zealand, and South Africa and later joined by the United States and the Soviet Union.

anti-Semitism: Hatred towards and discrimation against Jews.

Arbeitsdienst: National Labor Service, six months of unpaid labor, required of young people when they reached eighteen.

Aryan: Pseudoscientific theory used by the Nazis and other racists to falsely claim the Nazis a "master race." According to the Nazis, Aryans were superior to all others.

autobahn: Superhighway system built under Adolf Hitler.

BBC: British Broadcasting Corporation.

blitzkrieg: Lightning-like military attack.

Book burning: May 10,1933; The public burning through-out Germany of books labeled degenerate by the Nazis and thus unsuitable for Germans to read.

boycott: An organized campaign to stop people from buying from a particular group for racial, ethnic, or religious reasons.

Brownshirts: Members of a Nazi terrorist organization, the Storm Troopers, or S.A., Sturm Abteilungen.

Buchenwald: One of the first concentration camps. Over 200,000 perished there.

Communists: A political party.

concentration camps: Built by the Nazis regime to imprison people they considered undesirable. Millions died of starvation or disease or were murdered in gas chambers.

Confessing Church: Branch of Protestant church opposed to Hitler.

Conscientious objector: A person who does not believe in war for religious or moral reasons and who refuses to be inducted into the armed forces. In Allied nations, conscientious objectors were permitted to do alternative service, such as serving in hospitals and mental institutions. In Germany, conscientious objectors were killed.

Crystal Night: A nationwide pogrom against the Jews on November 9 and 10, 1938. In their destruction of Jewish homes, synagogues, and stores, the attackers littered the streets with broken glass. Hence the name, Kristalnacht, Night of the Broken Glass.

Dachau: Among the first concentration camps, built in 1933. In Dachau over 40,000 people were murdered, among them Jews, political prisoners, homosexuals, and priests.

Einsatzgruppen: S.S. units assigned to follow army units to murder Jews and others, such as Poles and gypsies, who were labeled undesirable by the Nazis.

ersatz: Substitute product, as in *ersatz coffee* made from bark.

Fliegerkorps: Flying corps to train young people to operate gliders.

führer: German for "leader;" title held by Adolf Hitler.

gauleiter: Nazi head of a district or *gau*.

Gestapo: Secret police organization in Germany. Shortened form of Geheimstattspolizei (secret state police). Known for its brutality in smashing opposition to the Nazi regime.

Göbbels, Josef: Minister of propaganda in the Nazi regime.

Göring, Hermann: Reichsmarshal and minister of aviation in the Nazi regime.

Heil Hitler: Nazi salute: "Hail, Hitler."

Hindenburg, Paul von: President of Germany. He appointed Adolf Hitler as chancellor of Germany.

Hitler, Adolf (1889-1945): dictator of Germany, 1933-1945.

Hitler Youth: Nazi organization created to indoctrinate German youth.

hochverrat: A law concerning the charge of treason. *Hochverrat* was defined as an attempt to overthrow the government for reasons of personal belief and first carried a penalty of three to five years. In 1943, the penalty was changed to the death sentence.

landesverrat: An act of treason. It was defined as an attempt to overthrow the government on behalf of a foreign power. It carried the death penalty.

Lao-Tsu: a Chinese philosopher.

Luftwafffe: German air force.

master plan: A plan to dominate the world by wiping out or enslaving various national, religious, and racial groups.

master race: Nazis claimed because they were Aryans they were superior to all other groups, making them a master race.

Munich Pact: A diplomatic agreement which gave the Sudetenland, a part of Czechoslovakia, to Germany.

Nazi: Political party, Nationalsozialistiche Deutsche Arbeiterpartei (National Socialist German Workers' party). Nazi is the shortened form.

Panzer: German tanks.

Ploetzensee Prison: A military prison in Berlin where executions took place.

pogrom: (Russian word). An organized massacre of helpless people, usually Jews.

Radio Orange: Offical Dutch radio station.

Reichstag: German parliament.

resistance: Secret underground movement against a political power.

Royal Air Force: British air force.

S.A.: Storm Troopers (*see* Brownshirts.)

scapegoat: Person who is blamed for someone else's misfortune.

Slavs: Peoples of Eastern European origin, such as Poles, Russians, Yugoslavians, Czechs, and Ukrainians.

Social Democrats: A political party opposed to the Nazis.

S.S.: Abbreviation for Schutzstaffel. Hitler's bodyguards; functions later expanded to include intelligence, central security, policing actions and operating concentrations camps.

Stuka bombers: German planes which acted as dive bombers. They made a terrifying, shrieking noise.

Sudetenland: A part of Czechoslovakia.

swastika: An ancient sign used by the Nazis as their symbol.

synagogue: A Jewish house of prayer.

todeskandidat (TD): A person condemned to death.

Uncle Tom's Cabin: A nineteenth-century book about slavery in America.

underground: An illegal, secret resistance organization.

Untermensch: People the Nazis labeled subhuman, such as Jews, gypsies, and Slavic peoples.

Weimar Republic: Democratic government established after World War I and overthrown by the Nazis.

Bibliography:
Other Books of Interest on the Resistance in Germany

Unlike the occupied countries of Europe, where there were strong resistance movements, in Germany, only a few individuals attempted to oppose the Nazis. Those who did came chiefly from the ranks of Social Democrats, Communists, Jews, labor leaders, a few dissenting clergy, and the officers and civilians involved in the General's Plot to overthrow Hitler.

While there are many books written about Jewish resistance in Germany, the following list deals only with books in *English* on the resistance of *non-Jews* in Germany.

The starred books were written for young adults. The others, while written for adult audiences, provide background information.

Bethge, Eberhard. *Costly Grace: An Illustrated Biography of Dietrich Bonhoeffer.* New York: Harper & Row, 1979.

*Cowan, Lore. *Children of the Resistance* last story, "Not Every German Is a Nazi." New York: Archway Paperback, 1971.

*Forman, James. *Ceremonies of Innocence.* New York: Hawthorn Books, 1970.

*Forman, James. *The Traitor.* New York: Hawthorn Books, 1970.

*Friedman, Ina. *The Other Victims: First-Person Stories of Non-Jews Persecuted by the Nazis.* Boston: Houghton Mifflin, 1990.

Hanser, Richard. *A Noble Treason: The Revolt of the Munich Students against Hitler.* New York: Putnam, 1979.

Hoffmann, Peter. *The History of the German Resistance Movement, 1933-1945*. Cambridge: MIT Press, 1977.

Moltke, Helmut, Graf von *Letters to Freya, 1939-1945*. Edited by Beate Ruhm von Open. New York: Knopf, 1990.

*Scholl, Inge. *Students against Tyranny: Munich, 1942-1943*. Translated from German by Arthur R. Schultz. Middleton, Conn.: Wesleyan University Press, 1970.

Snyder, L. Louis, *Hitler's German Enemies: Portraits of Heroes Who Fought the Nazis*. New York: Hippocrene Press, 1990.

*Vinke, Hermann. *The Short Life of Sophie Scholl*. New York: Harper & Row, 1984.

Wise, Robert, *The Pastors' Barracks*. Wheaton, Ill: SP Publications, 1986.

Zassenhaus, Hiltgunt. *Walls: Resisting the Third Reich-One Woman's Story*. Boston, Ma.: Beacon Press, 1974.

INDEX

Author and Artist Biographies

photo: Toledo Blade

Ina R. Friedman has explored the impact of the Nazi regime on the lives of young people in three books. Her first, *Escape or Die: True Stories of Young People Who Survived the Holocaust* describes the courageous and desperate steps young Jews took to escape from the Nazis. Her second book, *The Other Victims: First Person Stories of non-Jews Persecuted by the Nazis*, an ALAYAD "Best Books" and an ABA "Pick of the List," examines the Nazis' attempt to create a master race by wiping out so called "defective traits" and the human suffering caused by the Nazis' policies. In this third book, *Flying against the Wind: The Story of a Young Woman Who Defies the Nazis*, she relates the story of a young German Christian who refuses to accept the hatred and violence of the Nazis. Though she pays a terrible price for her resistance, she remains undefeated in spirit.

Ina R. Friedman has also written two books on the theme of cultural understanding. Her Reading Rainbow picture book, *How My Parents Learned to Eat*, received a Christopher Award for promoting cultural understanding. Her book, *Black Cop*, tells the story of a young man who rose from the ghetto to become deputy chief of the Washington, D.C. police force.

Ms. Friedman holds a B.A. from Penn State University and an M.A. from Lesley College in storytelling. She lives in Brookline, MA. and lectures throughout the United States.

Cover artist and book designer Michael Lenn (Mischa as he prefers to be called) has a masters degree from the Mukhina College of Art and Design in his native St. Petersburg, Russia. Since coming to the United States in 1990 he has had many commissions as a graphic artist and illustrator and has received an award for his textbook illustrations. In addition to his success as a graphic artist, Misha has had several exhibitions of his water colors. He resides in Boston, MA.

ORDER FORM

Flying Against the Wind

THE STORY OF A YOUNG WOMAN WHO DEFIED THE NAZIS

"A powerful biography of a young girl's coming-of-age in Nazi Germany ... relating not ony Cato's story of courage and compassion but also that of her mother and aunt. A role model for today's teenagers,"–Dr. Margot Stern Strom, director, Facing History and Ourselves.

Available through your local bookstore or through this order blank.

Please send ____ copies of *Flying against the Wind* (ISBN #1-886721-00-9) @ $11.95 U.S./ $14.95 Canada. Residents of Massachusetts please add 5% sales tax.

I am enclosing $_____,which includes $2.50 for shipping for the first book. For each additional book please add $1.00 for shipping. Send check or money order (no cash or C.O.D.s).

Mr./Ms._____

Address_____

City/State/Zip_____

Remit to: **Lodgepole Press**
PO Box 1259
Brookline, MA. 02146

Please allow 4 to 6 weeks for delivery.
SAN: 298-5012